60+? Get Ready t

Achieve Your Heyday, and Do It Your own Way!

60+? Get Ready to Rock

Achieve Your Heyday, and Do It Your own Way!

Audrey McIlvain

Published by Falt Ruadh Books

A CIP catalogue record for this book is available from the British Library.

The author has made every effort to provide accurate references and Internet addresses. If any have been inadvertently overlooked, the publisher will endeavour to make the necessary arrangements at the first opportunity. Neither the publisher nor the author assumes any responsibility for changes to Internet addresses that occur after publication.

ISBN 978-0-9570500-0-6

Book and cover design by Clare Brayshaw

Prepared and printed by:

York Publishing Services Ltd
64 Hallfield Road
Layerthorpe
York YO31 7ZQ

Tel: 01904 431213

Website: www.yps-publishing.co.uk

CONTENTS

About the Author

Audrey McIlvain has worked within the field of education for 37 years, first as a Primary School teacher and Assistant Head Teacher, later as a Teacher Trainer, Lecturer in Education and Psychology, and Consultant with the British Council. She has worked in the U.K., Spain, Mexico, South Africa and Chile. Audrey has published many articles and academic papers. She has also published seven children's books for Pearson Education. More recently, she has gained qualifications in Cognitive Behavioural Therapy, Mentoring, Coaching, and Stress Management. She now lives in Scarborough, North Yorkshire, where she works as a lecturer in Psychology with the Open University, guest speaker and writer. In her free time, she loves to sing, play her guitar and piano, write poetry and paint.

Acknowledgements

I am deeply indebted to Betty Carter (84), Helmsley, North Yorkshire, who provided the initial (and continued) inspiration and impetus to research and write this book.

In addition to Betty (referred to as Betty C. in the book), the other role models who participated in the research were (in alphabetical order by first name):

Ann Golder (72), Scarborough, North Yorkshire; Betty Smith (78) (referred to as Betty S. in the book), Scarborough; Christina (Chrissie) Scott (88), Moray, Scotland; D. (who prefers to remain 'incognito') (79), Moray, Scotland; Dorothy Jones (77), Scarborough (now living in Pickering); Elizabeth Waddell (79), Kirkintilloch, Glasgow; Isabel Ross (79), Kirkintilloch; Janet Turner (78), Pickering, North Yorkshire; Jessie Robertson (79), Kirkintilloch; Joanna Griffin (80), Scarborough; Kate Owens (83), Kirkintilloch; Mary Hannah (82), Kirkintilloch; Maureen Robinson (73), Scarborough; Norma Cochrane (86), Illinois, U.S.A.; Rusty Booth, Texas, U.S.A.; Shelagh Ogilvie Chamberlain (84), Scarborough; Susan Dressel-Myers (80), New Mexico, U.S.A.; Sue Sutherland (78) (referred to as Sue S. in the book), Florida, U.S.A., and Vera Cameron (83), Bishopbriggs, Glasgow.

I would like to express my sincere thanks to you all for your time, inspiration and patience throughout the research process. You are amazing people!

In addition, many thanks to Neil Anderson for putting me in touch with the wonderful research participants from Kirkintilloch and Bishopbriggs, and for being such a great support and source of encouragement throughout the project.

And, for providing me with the 'younger angle' on their hopes, dreams, fears and ideas concerning old age: Anita Collins, Annie Davies, Annie Hughes, Caroline Fanshawe, Ciara Boyes, Jane Berry, Karen John, Linda McGhie, Mark and Teresa Giles, Mira Kubecka, Neil Anderson, Sally Bissoni, Sam Peters and Zoe Hamlet da Silva. I hope you find the book useful when you are 'senior' enough to read it!

Many thanks also to Ketyn Jepson, Christine McKay and Cliff Bashforth for your very valuable contributions to my project.

To my dear friends Dr Joe Sutherland, Michael Wilson and Aubrey Banks, thank you for your insights and words of wisdom over the years I have known you.

Last, but not least, thank you, Tim, my darling husband, for all your help and patience with formatting, indents and all the technical stuff which is largely a mystery to me! What would I do without you?

Introduction

How To Get the Best Out of Reading and Using This Book

Take a few moments to consider why you are attracted to the book.

Perhaps you are approaching retirement and need to contemplate how to prepare for your 'golden years'? Maybe you are worried or even fearful about old age and what it might bring? Are there changes which you know would be of benefit, but you need some incentives to help you to move forward? Possibly you already know some people in their 70's and older who seem to live life to the full, and you would like to gain some insights into how you can do the same. Or, are you already in your 70's and you wish to improve some aspect of your lifestyle? Maybe there is a mixture of reasons why you picked up this book. Jot down your immediate thoughts below-this will help you to plan your goals later in the book.

I am reading this book because I want (or need) to:

There is a Buddhist saying which goes, "When the pupil is ready, s/he finds the teacher."

I am going to assume that you are ready for the **work** which this book requires if you are going to benefit fully from it. Unlike most books we read, this book is designed to be written on, highlighted, underlined, and used, to enable you to clarify the way forward in your life. There are exercises and activities to do in each chapter, and I strongly recommend that you complete these, either in the book or in a separate notebook. You may also wish to keep a journal to record and clarify your thoughts, wants, and needs as you work through the material.

Some of you may prefer to read through the book to get the overall gist of it first and then return to the key chapters which you feel will be of greatest benefit. Others may prefer to select a few chapters which seem most important to you and return to the others later. There really is no one way to engage with this book. You choose how you wish to proceed.

Alone or with others?

The book is designed to be used flexibly. You can work through it on your own. Alternatively, I have written the book in a style which can be easily adapted for group work (perhaps in a home-study group of friends, University of the Third Age, a taught course led by a tutor, etc). Or, you could team up with a friend to offer each other support and encouragement in a co-mentoring arrangement. If you are seeing a therapist, the activities and issues raised by the book may be useful to discuss when you meet with him or her.

Prioritise one or two goals to work on

Rather than rushing headlong into major changes, I recommend that you select a few realistic, achievable goals to work on over the next few months, and then review your progress. You can then add new goals or modify existing ones. The danger of trying to do too much too quickly is that we can lose momentum and give up altogether. (Think of the 'Hare and Tortoise' story.)

You can also return to this book after a few months or even years as your circumstances change. It is always useful to do a 'life audit' every now and again; this can galvanise us into action so that we can reap the benefits of each phase of our lives.

How the book is organised:

a) In each chapter, I will review the **findings from my research** which was based on open-ended questionnaires and semi-structured interviews with 20 women, aged between 70 and 88, drawn from a wide range of educational backgrounds. They had been identified by me, or by one of their friends, as **role models** – people who are living life to the full and flourishing in their 'golden years'. Some of them were well-known to me before this project started, and they are people whom I greatly admire for their vitality, wisdom, wonderful company and the very positive attitudes they seem to exude, even in the face of difficulty. Others, I have had the privilege and great pleasure of getting to know via their questionnaires and follow-up interviews. I was curious to know their secrets, and to give them an opportunity to pass on their wisdom and insights to a wider audience.

All too often, elderly people in our Western societies are marginalised, ignored and made to feel invisible. The images we see in the media tend to portray old age in a very negative way. More recently, reports focus on the growing (so-called) *'problem'* of an ageing population, completely ignoring the rich wisdom, experience and knowledge which we could all tap into and benefit from. It is interesting to compare this process with other societies where the elderly are revered, respected and fully integrated within their communities. In Okinawa, for example, people say: *'The elderly are our treasure.'* I wanted to give these marvellous role models a voice and, just as I predicted, I have learned a great deal from them that I wish to integrate within my own lifestyle. In addition, many of my anxieties about growing older have been addressed and appeased. Now, I want to share my findings with you so that you, too, can benefit.

b) We will also be examining **published research** into each of the topics covered by the book. As my research sample is relatively small, it is important to compare what I have discovered with findings from researchers in much larger projects, including longitudinal studies. I have provided a list of **sources for further reading** at the end of the book so that you can read about these topics in greater depth later if you wish to.

c) But, where this book really differs from other publications on ageing is that you will then **work out your own strategies** (with my help) to learn to implement the research findings in your own life. I see this as a preparation for easing your way into the transition between middle age and old age when that time comes. From my investigations, I believe that looking forward and being proactive in a practical way will help us to make more informed decisions about how we can enjoy our 'golden chapter' and find it fulfilling. We prepare for other important transitions such as going to University, entering the world of work, marriage, new jobs, parenthood. It makes sense to do the same before we enter the third age. Therefore, we will target diverse aspects of our lives: our thinking; exercise; diet; relationships; brain and memory; time management, etc. I hope you see this as an opportunity to manage your lifestyle ever more effectively which will pay dividends when you reach old age.

Be warned- hard work is involved

There are no quick fixes or promises of magic. Merely reading the book will not suffice. You will benefit only by applying yourself to the goals you set. But, your efforts will be richly rewarded when you witness the positive changes taking place in your life as the new (or currently dormant) strategies you practise gradually become an integral part of your everyday lifestyle.

This book is not about:

- Finding the secret to eternal youth – a futile quest;
- Time standing still – we have to learn to manage the transitions and changes in our lives with grace and fortitude;

- Looking young for ever – you can't –simple!
- Medical, legal or financial matters as they are outside my field;
- The complex debate about assisted dying and euthanasia – these subjects require a book of their own to analyse them adequately;
- Longevity, although that will be discussed. In Abraham Lincoln's famous words: *"In the end, it's not the years in your life that count. It's the life in your years."*

Imagine for a moment what it would be like if we were to let go of the endless quest to look young forever. Think of the money and time we would save. Consider how liberating it would be to treasure our laughter lines as evidence that we have lived a full and happy life instead of the endless quest to find some magic potion to keep them at bay.

The cult of youth which predominates today seems to keep too many people in a time-warp based on an infantile state of arrested development. (Think of some of the celebrities as examples of this.) Therefore, the word *'young'* is not used in relation to goals or strategies we might wish to strive towards at any point in this book. Instead, you will find reference to words such as: vibrant, relevant, wise, flourishing, vital, radiant, resilient and serene. These are states which we can **all** aspire to with a bit of effort and know-how.

Find your own, unique pathway:

All the ladies in my research (hereafter referred to as ***'the participants'***), glow from within, and this is because they have learned how to make the most of this time of their lives. But, they are all unique individuals (with strengths and weaknesses) who have found their **own** way in life: there is no one 'recipe' which works for everyone because we are all so different. As my dear friend, Michael Wilson (now in his late 70's), said to me when I asked him about his views on how to age well: *"There are at least 62 million people living in the UK. That means there are 62 million different ways of ageing well!!!"* The participants have made their own choices which work for them.

Now, you can learn how to do this too, embracing the future with increased confidence, positive attitudes, resilience and relevant practical information. Achieve your heyday, and do it your own way!

* * * * *

Note: Before you begin reading, I recommend that you complete the questionnaire in Appendix 1. This will provide a useful baseline and help you to identify where your strengths and 'targets' currently lie. It will also help you to monitor goals, developments and achievements as you work through the book. This questionnaire is similar to the one the participants filled in before their interviews with me, but I have adapted it to be more useful for your personal project and action plan.

1 Manage Your Thinking

Betty Carter offered a well-known quote in her response to my questions about how to deal with negative thoughts and fears:

> ***"Two men look out through the same prison bars. One sees the mud, the other stars."*** *(Rev. Frederick Langbridge (1849-1923)*

This was a recurrent theme in the participants' answers, and I found they all had well-defined strategies to help them cope with life's ups and downs, negative thoughts and their fears. Ageing well is not just about our physical selves or our appearance: our state of mind plays a crucial role in how we experience old age.

Betty Carter

The practical strategies used regularly by the participants included:

Distraction

Very often, engaging in an activity such as going for a walk, phoning a friend, going shopping, doing some painting (both house decorating and picture painting) was mentioned by participants as a coping mechanism when negative thoughts surface. This strategy is often recommended by cognitive behavioural therapists. The rationale behind it is that when we are busy with some engaging activity, we become absorbed so we stop brooding.

Expressing gratitude for what we have

The practice of gratefulness was mentioned by many. For example, Betty S. tells herself: *"Be content with your lot in life"* when she feels a bit down. Similarly, Janet, who suffered a 'close call' in her 30s, reminds herself that *"I am lucky to be alive."*

Martin Seligman (2003), who is regarded as the person who initiated 'positive psychology' strongly advocates the practice of gratitude. What his research demonstrates is that we need to appreciate and savour the good things in our lives. If we focus too much on the bad things, that can undermine our serenity and well-being.

Looking forward rather than backwards

Betty C. sums this up succinctly when she says, *"Don't cling on to past heartaches. Learn from them and look forward to new adventures."*

Similarly, Betty S. advises, *"Live each day separately, and don't look back."*

Betty Smith

I was impressed by the complete lack of bitterness, grudges or resentment that I found in the participants. They had all had their ups and downs, but there is a **resilience** which has developed through learning from these experiences. This brings to mind a book written by Dr. Robert Schuller (1983), the title of which is: *"Tough times never last, but tough people do."*

Such views are echoed in Robert Dilts' research (1992) of people who had retained their vitality in old age in Holland. There, he found the best role models all viewed the trials and tribulations of life as an opportunity to develop.

Howard Friedman and Leslie Martin (2011) discovered that people who had learned from their parents' mistakes and resolved to do things differently were not only able to flourish in later life, but they also benefited in the long run. This is very encouraging to those of us whose parents were not very effective role models and, perhaps, we fear that our lives (and our health) may turn out the same. In their Longevity Project, Howard Friedman and Leslie Martin discovered that those who grappled with the challenge, and grew stronger as a result, went on to live long lives.

A well-known example of someone who has learned how to change is Nelson Mandela who refused to allow bitterness and hatred to prevail after his release from prison: instead, he led his people forward in a spirit of reconciliation. One only has to look at his face now to bear witness to the inner peace he has derived from this insight.

And, isn't that something we will all wish to have in our later years- inner peace and serenity?

Seeking solutions

The participants actively demonstrate their desire to find a solution to their problems rather than allow problems or catastrophising to engulf them.

For example, one lady's husband left her for another woman, and she had two young sons to fend for. With no hint of self-pity, she told me, *"So I had to find something that I could do."* She weighed up all her options and found work which could fit around the boys' schooling. Needless to say, she never looked back.

Again and again, the other participants told me of similar experiences: when faced with a crisis, they look for their best option. This calls to mind a wonderful sermon delivered in Church by my dear friend, Dr Joe Sutherland (Sue S.'s husband). I was going through a terrible time in my own life, and, in his sermon, Joe told us that the Chinese symbol for *'crisis'* also means *'opportunity'.* I realised then that I had to think creatively about what opportunity my current (dire) circumstances were offering to me, weigh up the pros and cons of each option, and move forward in my life.

Joe Sutherland

In a recently published book by Steve Taylor, *'Out of the Darkness'* (2011), he uses the term, *'shifters',* to describe people who have hit 'rock bottom', but emerge with a better sense of well-being and a rekindled sense of purpose. I can certainly recognise that pattern both in myself and in the participants. Being adaptable, able to think on our feet and let go of things which no longer serve us well, clears the ground for new, better things to enter our lives. We literally have to *'shift'* perspective.

Robert Dilts (1992) found in his study of active, elderly role models, that they had all gone through traumatic or difficult times at some stage in their lives. However, they had dealt with their difficult times resourcefully, and he concludes that this was the *'difference that made a difference'*. Finding solutions to the challenges and traumas of life seems to be a key feature of those who develop the inner strength, creativity and resilience which we will all need in our old age. To quote the words of the German philosopher, Nietzsche: *'What does not destroy me makes me stronger.'*

Talking things over with friends

Ann commented, *"When I am feeling down, talking to my friends over lunch is all the support I need."*

It is well-documented elsewhere that female friendships play a vital role in women's emotional lives. What I also found in the participants was that many of their friendships have endured over 50 years, and with these trusted key people to share with and confide in, problems could be addressed more easily. This is an important theme to which we return more fully in Chapter 6.

Which of these strategies do you use? Which strategies might help you to deal with life and all that comes our way?

The common thread that emerges from my research project and from published research is that **how we respond and react to events** (especially those events over which we have little or no control) shapes our thinking over the years, and patterns of thinking can become habits which are difficult to change. In the words of the Talmud:

'We do not see the world as it is. We see the world as we are.'

Within the context of ageing, this has particular significance. Thomas Hess (2003) found that, when older people were told something positive about ageing before they carried out memory tests (e.g. there is not much of a decline in memory in old age), they performed better than if they were told something negative about ageing (e.g. the study is about how ageing affects memory). (Cited in Strauss, 2010)

Ellen Langer (2010) refers to this process as 'priming'. Thus, if we are told what is expected of us, we tend to comply without even being aware of it. The world of advertising uses this strategy all the time. She recounts an experiment in which one group of elderly people were given anagrams to solve which had stereotypes of words such as 'felorguft' for 'forgetful'. The other group (the control) was given neutral, non-age related words for their clues. After the experiment, the participants were observed. Those people who had to solve the anagrams related to negative stereotypes of 'old age' walked to the lift more slowly!

Becca Levy (2002) found that people who were shown negative words about ageing (e.g. decline, dementia, confused, decrepit) performed less well in the memory tests that followed than the group who were shown positive words (e.g. wise, alert, learned, sage) before they were tested. (Cited in Strauss, 2010)

So, choose your newspaper, magazines, television programmes with care. Notice how priming is all around us, and scrutinise your own attitudes to become aware of negative thinking and expectancy which can infiltrate your mindset.

Now, returning to Betty C.'s quote, which would you prefer to be- a 'star-gazer' or a 'mud-watcher'?

Activities to help you become a 'star-gazer':

Become mindful

Monitor your thoughts for a whole day. On the hour, every hour, write down exactly how you are feeling and what you are thinking. Note what you are doing at the time. (The photocopiable chart in Appendix 3: '*Monitoring your time, thoughts and feelings*' will be useful.) Be totally honest with yourself!

Are there any **patterns** of thinking? Do you tend towards negative or fearful thoughts? Were you surprised by the results?

Do any of the following apply to you?

Self-blame – do you tend to blame yourself for things which are not your fault? A common symptom of self-blame is that you find yourself constantly apologising even when, deep down, you know you are not to blame;

Personalisation – this is when you take things to heart or think they are directed at you when they are not. For example, if the boss is in a foul mood, you think you must have done something to upset him or your work is not up to scratch;

Mind reading – perhaps you impute motives or you jump to conclusions about what other people are thinking, but there is no evidence to support your conclusions. For example, a friend is rather quiet and preoccupied, and you think, 'She is so bored with me';

Over-generalisation – if you frequently use words such as 'always', 'never', 'every', 'nobody', you are probably over-generalising (e.g. 'I never get things right', 'I always screw up');

Perfectionism – do you think you have to do everything perfectly in order to be acceptable? Do you set yourself such high standards that you are afraid of trying new things? Do you beat yourself up over tiny mistakes? Do you fret over choices to the point of not taking any action at all?

Catastrophising – do you think things are much worse than they really are? Do you launch into 'worst case scenario' mode at the slightest hiccup?

Selective seeing – do you have a tendency to see only the negative things around you and ignore the good things? Do you tend to recall only your mistakes and ignore your successes? Do you worry constantly about the future and only focus on what might go wrong?

Identify the causes

What are the events or people (past or present) contributing to your **positive** thoughts and feelings? Try to spend even more time with these people and in these situations as they are beneficial to you.

What are the situations and people to which you are responding less positively? Often, these patterns can be traced back to childhood events. If this is the case and you know you would benefit from talking this through, do not hesitate to seek help from a qualified professional. (See 'Useful Contacts'.) If you prefer a 'self-help' approach, the book by Stephen Briers listed under 'Sources' may help. If you have access to the internet, try the free online exercises at www.llttf.com ('Living Life to the Full').

Here are some strategies to try if you find your habitual thoughts are negative or dysfunctional. They are often used by Cognitive Behavioural Therapists:

Practise 'thought stopping' techniques. Become aware of when you lapse into any of the dysfunctional habits above and say aloud (very firmly): **"Stop that!"** or **"No!"** Then apply some of the strategies below to try to break the pattern. This will take time, persistence and application because, very often, these habitual patterns have been with us for a long time, but conscious effort will pay dividends.

Place 'post-its' (or coloured 'dots') around your home to remind you to be aware of what you are thinking and how these thoughts are affecting your emotions. This can help prevent you lapsing into a 'default setting' of negative or dysfunctional thinking without being aware that you are doing so. When you notice the post-it or dot, stop and notice you thoughts and feelings. Then take action-

Try to replace the negative or dysfunctional one with a more positive, realistic one. For example, "Everything is going wrong today" (over-generalisation and perfectionism) can be replaced by listing all the things that have gone 'right' or 'well enough' today. That will help you to gain a better, more realistic sense of perspective.

Or, if you are thinking, "Sheila hasn't called me. She must have fallen out with me" (mind-reading) replace that thought with a more realistic one such as, "Sheila might be really busy, or maybe she is unwell. I'll ring her to find out."

Do a reality check. Is there any **evidence** for your thoughts? How **realistic** are they? How **likely** is this to happen? Would **another person** see this situation in the same way? Are my thoughts making things worse than they **really are?**

Do something active. As the participants have discovered, throwing yourself into an activity which is sufficiently absorbing will distract you and get you thinking about something else. (This can include more sedentary pastimes such as crosswords or embroidery for those who can't move around so well.)

In the words of the gardener, Ben, in Frances Hodgson Burnett's classic book, *'The Secret Garden': "Where you tend a rose, my lad, a thistle cannot grow."*

Whatever happens, try not to sit for lengthy periods of time, staring into space, or watching something mindless on TV. That is a recipe for going into our default setting of negative or dysfunctional thinking.

Keep a gratitude diary. Every day, record all the good things you are grateful for. A useful time to do this is before you go to sleep as this will calm your mind and induce relaxed feelings to help you to drift off. Aim to find at least **three** things each day to be genuinely grateful for.

And, as Martin Seligman (2003) recommends, let people know how grateful you are to them. This can be verbally, or, even better, in a letter of gratitude which you read to them in which you tell them all the positive things they have brought into your life.

Let go of bitterness – it eats you up inside. While it can be difficult to forgive those who have done us an injury in the past, moving on and not allowing resentment to fester within us is well-documented by many research studies as essential to our emotional well-being in later life. If we allow bitterness and hatred to prevail, the only person who really suffers is – **ourselves**. Don't forget that our faces reveal what we feel inside as we age. Do you want to look bitter and angry on the outside when you are 70?

Some people seem to almost delight in dwelling on past hurts and disappointments, but, as my friend, Christine McKay, said to me the other day, *"We wouldn't dream of reading the same chapter in a book over and over, would we? So, we have to accept the past is in the past, and look forward to the next chapter of our lives."*

Distinguish between those things we can control and those we cannot. Do you remember the 'Serenity Prayer'? It must have sold thousands of copies worldwide, reproduced on fridge magnets, cards, and trinkets. Yet the words are just as powerful today. For younger readers who may not know the prayer (and to remind the rest of us), here it is:

> ***"Lord, grant me the serenity to accept the things I cannot change, the courage to change the things I can, and the wisdom to know the difference."***

(For those who are 'non-believers', just use the verse as a motivator, and start with 'grant'.)

Most of us would like to embark on the 'golden chapter' serenely and I was interested in 90 year-old, Dr. Stanley Karansky, who is featured in Norman Doidge's book: *'The Brain That Changes Itself'* (2007), because he is so lively, active and always on the lookout for new experiences. When Norman Doidge commented to him that he seems much less anxious and agitated than most people, Dr. Karansky explained that there are many things that could affect him, but they are outside his control. So, instead, he focuses his attention on how he responds to them.

Betty C. was put to the test recently when she had to undergo a serious medical procedure. But, in true Betty style, she told the hospital consultant; *"Well, I'm on stage now, so I'll have to dance, won't I?"* The consultant informed her that most people, half her age, would have crumpled at the very idea of what she had to face. She has now recovered and is enjoying life to the full again. It does seem that being able to 'see the stars' can help us through the challenges which we will **all** have to face at some time in our old age.

Similarly, a lovely elderly friend of mine, Aubrey Banks, had to have chemotherapy and radiotherapy a few months ago, but he faced it with fortitude and found the inner strength to cope, saying, *"Well, you just have to get on with it, don't you?"* He has now been given the 'all clear', and I find his countenance radiates with inner peace and gratitude.

I only hope that we can all find the inner resources that Betty and Aubrey have discovered in themselves when our time of challenge comes.

There are many other strategies which you can try and a plethora of self-help books to assist us in our quest to conquer negative thinking and acquire a more serene outlook on life, but this old joke reminds us of one key factor:

How many psychotherapists does it take to change a light-bulb?
Answer: only one but it has to want to change.

Yes, we can learn to think differently and more healthily, but there is work and effort involved in changing our patterns from the past. As Norman Doidge (2007) explains, when we acquire a bad habit, it takes over a map in our brain. Then, every time we repeat it, it assumes more control over that map. That is why it is so important to replace dysfunctional thoughts with better ones. It also helps us to understand why 'unlearning' can require so much hard work over a considerable timeframe. If you want to, you can, but only you can do it. And, the good news is **you can**. When you read about the 'plasticity' of the brain in Chapter 7, you will see why. So, don't give up- you can change your light bulb if you really want to. But, as Betty C. has found, *"You have to make it happen. It's not going to come and find you."*

Let's finish with a reassuring quote from participant, Susan Dressel-Myers. When I asked what she thinks are the best things about growing older, she responded:

Susan Dressel-Myers

"I think that the most valuable benefit of ageing is PERSPECTIVE. It seems easier to know what's really important in life now."

That's something to look forward to!

Do this activity after you identify any patterns of thinking you wish to change:

Something I am going to change in the way I think is...

I will do this by using these strategies:

-
-
-

I will know I am successful when...

> **And...SING!** In the bath, in the car – anywhere! Just sing at the top of your voice, and, like the participants in Robert Dilts' research (1992), you will soon feel better. When you are singing an upbeat, happy song, it is impossible to dwell on negative thinking or your fears.

2 Release Your Zest for Life

Betty Carter provided the initial inspiration for me to write this book: every time I am in her company, I come away feeling energised and inspired by her tremendous zest for life.

But what is 'zest'? Is it something some people are born with? Can we all learn to gain more of it in our own lives? We all know it when we experience it, either in ourselves or in others, and I believe we can 'unbundle' and discover how to inject it into our daily lives.

Let's start by defining it. My trusty Collins Dictionary and Thesaurus defines zest as: 'something added to give flavour, interest or relish.' I like the sound of that! The Thesaurus suggests as synonyms: appetite, gusto, relish, zeal, zing, spice, tang and enjoyment. All of these have very positive connotations for me- how about you? Are you up for the challenge?

What gives the participants their zest for life?

One of the key reasons why the participants were selected is because they all seem to relish living. With few exceptions, the people I interviewed told me that **this** time is the best time of their lives and they are making the most of it. As Betty C. said, *"Any time is the best time in your life, but you have to make it happen!"*

However, they vary in the form their zest takes and they express it in different ways. This will be a recurring theme throughout this book: we are all unique individuals and we have to find our own way forward.

Here are their responses to my questions about what gives them their zest for life:

Family, friends and relationships come first by a <u>long</u> way. Other diverse sources include: days out, my home, good health, looking forward to each day, meeting people and sharing experiences, getting up in the morning, Christian faith, putting on my make-up, having wide interests and hobbies, keeping life simple with as few pressures as possible, having something to get dressed and go out for, the enthusiasm of grandchildren and young people, the beautiful Yorkshire countryside, inspiring music, the wonder of nature, art, painting, walking in the countryside, digging in the garden, variety (often said to be the spice of life), love of exercise, reading interesting books, and, finally, from Rusty, *"for the icing on the cake- one delicious latté a day!"*

As you can see, there is a wide variety there. What was also noteworthy is that no one identified money, wealth or materialistic things as a source of zest in their lives. For most people, it is the little things and the people they love that really count. However, some participants acknowledged that being 'comfortable' financially helps because it enables us to make more choices, a point we will return to presently.

Rusty Booth

So, what is <u>your</u> current zest rating?

On a scale of one to ten, one being 'life is humdrum, routine and dull', and ten being 'I have lots of zest in my life' where would you currently place yourself?

1 ______________________ 5 ______________________ 10

Which aspects of your life currently provide zest for you?

How might you improve on your zest rating? Here are some starting points to help you add more zing to your days:

a) Be open to serendipity:

Susan enjoys the fact that she can now be open to serendipity by not over-timetabling her days. Similarly, Isabel likes to be spontaneous if something turns up, rather than having a fixed routine, and Betty C. is always *"open to adventures."* Betty C. told me of the time a friend asked her to cruise to New York with her when Betty was in her 70's. At the time, Betty had not planned to go on holiday as some expenses had arisen, but she decided to go after all to keep her friend company. And there, at dinner, she met a lovely man, Franco, with whom she enjoyed the most romantic relationship which lasted for many years. She would not have missed it for anything. But, imagine how she would have missed out if she had avoided serendipity.

Isabel Ross

Undoubtedly, getting into a fixed routine which is dominated by 'must-do' chores is the quickest way to lose our zing. Betty C. also told me a good joke which sums this up: ***What is the difference between a groove and a grave? Only a matter of degree!***

What will YOU do to open yourself up more to serendipity?

Be flexible, open and ready for interesting things and people to come into your life, and they will!

b) Find interests and activities which totally absorb and engage you:

Mary Hannah

Mary describes her painting as providing complete immersion to the point where she is totally absorbed in what she is doing. All background noise and activity cease to be, and time seems to stand still.

What Mary is describing is termed **'flow'** by Mihaly Csikszentmihalyi (1990). Sometimes, athletes call it **'the zone'.** When we experience this state, as Daniel Goleman (1996) tells us, we feel energised and totally caught up in the activity. We engage in it just for the pleasure it gives us. After being in 'flow', we tend to feel satisfied, alive and vital. It enhances our feelings of well-being. Indeed, it may be an integral component in discovering zest in our lives.

What do you currently do to experience flow?

If you are drawing a blank on this one, think back to your childhood. Which activities and pastimes engaged you totally? When did you feel at your most vital? What gave you that buzz then? When did you lose yourself in something which brought you great satisfaction? It is time to rediscover some of those activities, and, most importantly, to **make time** for them. You will feel richly rewarded for doing so. (We will return to this theme in Chapter 9: Organise Your Time.)

How will you recreate more flow in your life?

c) GO, especially when you don't want to:

Refuse to give in to apathy and 'can't be bothered' attitudes. As Betty C. points out, *"When you get offers to go out, you MUST do it,* ***especially*** *if you feel tired. Once you have dressed and you get there, you will feel like a different person because you meet people, have a laugh and you stop thinking about yourself."*

Tim Drake and Chris Middleton (2009) suggest that, if we want to create more energy, first we have to use up the energy we already have. In other words, using energy creates new energy. Otherwise, we just feel stale and lethargic.

Think of role models you know who put this into practice. For Ann, it was a lady of 90+, and she told me, *"I could easily sit at home and do nothing, but when I feel like that I think of her and say to myself, if she could do it when she was in her 90's, so can I."*

Think of offers or occasions during the past month which you have turned down or made excuses not to attend. Visualise yourself if you had gone out, the people

you might have met, the interesting time you could have had. Even if it had turned out to be boring, at least you might have some funny stories to dine out on or amuse your friends with over coffee afterwards.

Ann Golder, husband Ken and Grandchildren

If, like me, you are rather shy, you may find yourself regularly avoiding social occasions, but that can become a vicious circle. It is only by going out and meeting people that we develop our social confidence, so just make yourself do it.

Plan some strategies to coax yourself into going out next time you 'can't be bothered'. If you want more zing in your life, you know you must get out there!

d) Conquer the fears which hold you back:

Think about Betty C. on her cruise to New York. Picture the night she met Franco. Visualise her visiting his home in New York afterwards, being wined and dined in style. Fast forward to the time they visited Venice and Paris together by rail, sipping champagne and feeling truly adored.

At any point in this story either Betty or Franco could have allowed fear and 'what if' thoughts to dominate. But, fortunately, they did not, and Betty and Franco will now hold on to those cherished memories for the rest of their lives.

Fear can trap us in dull routines and our comfort zones because we feel safe with the devil we know. But, think of all the things we can be missing out on if we always opt for the safe choice.

It is no surprise that Susan Jeffers' book, *'Feel the Fear and Do It Anyway'* (1987), has sold millions of books worldwide. If you have not read it and you think that fear is your main obstacle, grab a copy. Or, perhaps you read it a long time ago, and a revisit would be useful. I totally agree with her thesis which is that it is only by *'doing it anyway'* that we overcome the obstacles which fear puts in our way.

Usually, after we take the risk and face the challenge, we realise that our fear was greatly exaggerated in our minds. Of course, we all feel anxious or scared before making changes or trying out new ventures, but, at the same time, we need those new experiences to bring a buzz into our lives. Otherwise we become like cars which chug along in 2nd gear, never revving up to 5th to catch the excitement that life can bring to us at any age.

Sue Sutherland

For those participants with strong religious faith such as Sue S., Shelagh and Norma, there is a strong sense of their belief in a kind of *'universal goodness'* (to quote Drake and Middleton, 2009, p.176) which gives them strength and courage when new challenges present themselves. I have lost count of the number of times Sue and her husband, Joe, have said they were retiring from Church Ministry, but always a new mission presents itself and they rise to the challenge, their belief in God's calling guiding them forwards.

Betty S. also finds activities such as Yoga give her the confidence and strength to live fully day to day without worrying about the future.

How will you let go of fear which holds you back from fully 'dancing with the zest of life'? List a few things which you would love to do, but fear is preventing you, then plan what you could do to move towards your goals. Small steps forwards will get you there in the end. Don't forget to write the dates when you will take these steps. Keep these visible on your kitchen calendar. No excuses, please!

What I would love to do	What I am afraid of	One step I could take towards this goal is...	The next step could be...	And the next...

When I first started to imagine writing this book, fear almost took the upper hand, but how glad I am now that I managed to conquer it with Betty C.'s inspiration to motivate me. Now, you can do the same: conquer the fear which has held you back for too long.

e) Explore new things, new sensations, new sights and new people:

The participants demonstrated a remarkable degree of curiosity and a thirst for learning about the world. Let me provide some examples:

Mary is a keen artist, but, not content with mastering one technique, she is always on the lookout for new techniques and media. This leads her to different classes and groups with different tutors so that she can learn something new.

Elizabeth Waddell

Similarly, Elizabeth talks of *"keeping up to date and in touch"* while D. says how important it is to *"socialise and have fresh conversation to learn something new."*

Dorothy extols the virtues of having *"as many interests as one can"* and Susan's joie de vivre comes from being open to new sources of stimulation rather than *"rusting away."*

I could go on to cite many more examples, but the key point is that these ladies have an almost childlike, playful approach to novelty. Watch a child when he or she is given a new toy. They will use all their senses to explore and experience it fully: turning it round and round to see and feel its different features, smelling it, rattling it to hear if it makes a noise, and, invariably, tasting it. They don't wait to be told what to do with it in the way that we, as adults, tend to do when we attend a class or buy a new piece of equipment.

Perhaps one way of getting more zest in our lives is to reawaken all our senses:

- our taste buds- so eat or drink something you have never tried before;
- our sense of smell- try a new perfume or aromatherapy massage;
- listen to new music;
- explore new textures;
- visit new sights and,
- fully immerse ourselves in the sheer, sensual experience of novelty with a playful, unafraid, fresh delight.

When was the last time you tried something new? Is it time to have a go? Plan something to do THIS WEEK to stimulate all your senses.

Sense	What you could do	When	Where	With whom
Taste				
Smell				
Touch				
Sight				
Listening				
All of them!!				

The good thing, as the participants have discovered, is that most of the wonderful new experiences we can have cost very little. Indeed, in the world of nature, we have an ongoing sensory extravaganza for free. As the sculptor, Barbara Hepworth said: *'In the contemplation of nature we are perpetually renewed, our sense of mystery and our imagination is kept alive.'* (1934) **But this can only happen if we are switched on to receive it and engage with it.**

And, in order to do this, we have to be...

f) **Fully** present in the moment:

The other day I watched a young child eat an ice-cream cone. First, he looked at it this way and that, then he rolled his tongue, slowly and deliberately, around the bit that was melting down the side. Totally engrossed, he then started on the tip of the cone, tentatively lapping it and savouring the sensation of the delicious cool ice-cream on his lips and tongue. Throughout, he was totally in 'flow', oblivious to anything other than the sensory joy of this ice-cream. When did you last feel like that?

All too often, as adults, we are so preoccupied with busy thoughts, worries, plans and distractions that precious moments are over and gone while we have been mentally absent. Not so the participants! Norma talks of: *"Living fully in the present, and enjoying the moment."*

When Betty C. told me of her wonderful time in Paris with Franco, she recalled how she marvelled at the thrill of it all. As she sipped her champagne, *"I thought to myself- this is really happening to ME! NOW!"*

Perhaps, as we get older, we begin to realise how precious each day is. In Ann's words, *"Each day is a bonus to be enjoyed to the full."*

If we could learn to savour each day and the special moments within them, how much more fully we would relish our experiences.

Norma Cochrane & Dale

So, learn to calm and still your mind and those noisy, busy thoughts.

Breathe slowly and gently as you try out a new experience. As you exhale, let go of all tension.

Concentrate on what is happening to you, and focus on each of your senses in turn to engage fully and completely.

When you eat or drink, do it slowly, savouring each mouthful.

Avoid distractions by turning off the television or background music.

Remember, *you will never live this moment again,* so enter into it with all your heart and soul.

Find your inner tranquillity, and... just be.

g) Let go of guilt or feeling 'undeserving':

Many years ago, I read Shakti Gawain's bestseller, '*Creative Visualisation*' (1982). I was on a Consultancy in Kwa Zulu, South Africa at the time and I was battling with guilt that I had so much in my life while those around me were living in abject poverty with few prospects of improvement. Then I stumbled across one of her suggested affirmations where she reminds us that we inhabit a *'rich universe'*, so there is plenty for all of us.

I realised then that feeling guilty or undeserving was not going to serve any purpose. But, counting my blessings and feeling truly blessed would.

None of the participants professed any guilt or feelings of not deserving the good things in their lives, but they told me over and again (with no exceptions) how 'lucky', 'fortunate' and 'blessed' they feel, and how important it is to count our blessings every day. (See also Chapter 1.)

So, enjoy your pleasures, have fun, and let go of guilt which can entrap you in stultifying lifestyles and pursuits which drain you of zing and energy. Learning to value and feel grateful for everything you have will give you the kind of gusto we all need if we are to have zest in our lives. (If there are specific challenges in doing this, do consider talking it through with a qualified, registered therapist. See 'Useful Contacts'.)

h) Practise good sense as well as sensibility:

As I mentioned at the beginning of this chapter, having a financial 'cushion' will, of course, increase our comfort and the choices open to us when we are old.

Financial planning is beyond the scope of this book, but if you are wondering how you will fund all these lovely experiences, perhaps it is time to do an audit of your current expenditure. The only way to do this is to be brutally honest with yourself. Write down **every single thing that you spend money on in a month.** Keep receipts and tally up exactly where your money goes. When you have surveyed the total expenditure, divide the list into three columns:

ESSENTIALS	WANTS	WASTAGE

Essentials will include mortgage or rent, utilities, community tax, phone bills, etc. Wants will include all those things you **wanted** to buy, but were not really **essential.** Wastage includes the items which you bought on impulse, or when you squandered money mindlessly.

Now take time to consider where you could save money each month. **THE CARROT** is that you will find that you can afford to treat yourself to a zest-providing experience with the money you save.

This exercise is very empowering, because it puts you back in control, and there is no hiding place. You have to face up to your spending habits. It is also very satisfying to find ways to save money, even on essentials. Perhaps you can change your utilities providers, including your phone. Financial experts tell us we should do this auditing exercise regularly.

And, do think carefully about pensions and saving for the future. As my participants have all found: having a comfortable lifestyle in old age does enhance the zest quota! If you want to sip champagne in Paris when you are 80, best start saving now!

i) Imagine your last days:

What are the things you might wish you had done, or you never got round to doing? I'll wager your list does not contain any housework!!!

In Nadine Stair's poem, written when she was 85, she says:

I'd Pick More Daisies

If I had my life to live over,
I'd try to make more mistakes next time.
I would relax. I would limber up.
I would be sillier than I have on this trip.
I would be crazier. I would be less hygienic.
I would take more chances, I would take more trips.
I would climb more mountains, swim more rivers,
and watch more sunsets.
I would burn more gasoline. I would eat more ice cream and less beans.
I would have more actual troubles and fewer imaginary ones.
You see, I am one of those people who lives
prophylactically and sensibly and sanely,
hour after hour, day after day.

Oh, I have had my moments
And if I had it to do over again, I'd have more of them.
In fact, I'd try to have nothing else.
Just moments,one after another.
Instead of living so many years ahead each day.
I have been one of those people who never go anywhere
without a thermometer, a hot water bottle, a gargle, a
raincoat, and a parachute.

If I had to do it over again, I would go places and do things.
I'd travel lighter than I have.
If I had my life to live over, I would start barefooted
earlier in the spring and stay that way later in the fall.
I would play hooky more. I wouldn't make such good grades
except by accident.
I would ride on merry-go-rounds.

I'd pick more daisies!

How about you? What will you make sure you do?

Conclusion:

I hope this chapter and what the participants have shared has inspired you to get more zest in your life. Remember, this is **YOUR** life, and you have the right to live it your way.

And, isn't it comforting to know that we can look forward to a time when we feel even more liberated and full of zest if we can learn how to 'pick more daisies'? So, start today – **add life to your years!**

And... SING! When you sing your whole body vibrates and you feel more alive. So, sing everywhere you go- in the bath, in the car, when you're doing the housework, let rip. Here is a new slogan for you: ***If you want more ZING, you have to SING!!!!***

3 Enjoy the Way You Look at Any Age

At some point in our lives, most of us will have a strange encounter with a middle aged or elderly person. It may happen when we are in a shop trying on some clothes, when we are passing a shop window, or if someone has taken a photograph of us unexpectedly (i.e. before we have a chance to 'compose' our expression). We may think, "Oh, s/he looks familiar." Then, we realise that the person we are looking at is ourselves- not the youthful image we like to preserve in our memory, but the real person we have now become in our 50's, 60's and onwards.

For me, that moment arrived when I was about to go into hospital. As I never wear night attire, I had to purchase a nightgown. I will never forget the horror of seeing myself reflected in a shop mirror as I held a ghastly, frilly, pastel-coloured nightie against me and saw this image of my older self for the first time. My face also reflected the anxiety I was feeling about the complex operation I was about to face. "Who on earth is that, I gasped? Surely that's not me!" (You will be relieved to know that I opted for a long, slinky, black number instead!)

In this chapter, we will look afresh at ourselves, and take stock of what brings out the best in the way we look now. This will not be a futile search for 'eternal youth' or 'making time stand still', but it will involve learning to value our best attributes and make the most of those at every stage of our lives. Every phase we enter necessitates some rethinking about our style, for what can be worse than sticking with outdated clothes, hairstyles or make-up which no longer suit us, or make us look like 'mutton dressed as lamb'? (Or, even worse, *"mutton dressed as mutton"*, as Cliff Bashforth from 'Colour Me Beautiful' quipped when I interviewed him.)

I find it extremely depressing that so many people today seem to be on an endless quest to look eternally young, and I totally agree with Marie de Hennezel (2011) who writes of the infantile state people become imprisoned by when they become obsessed by trying to remain young for ever. She argues that, by doing so, they fail to prepare themselves for the transition into old age.

This appears to be a common preoccupation amongst the celebrity culture at the expense of finding their inner radiance and beauty, and feeling happy in the skin they are now in.

So, what did my participants think?

For the majority, daily grooming was a vital part of their day, and, as Shelagh said, *"Personal grooming is important because it's a pride in one's self."*

Betty Carter wrote, *"You can face anything if you are looking as good as possible. It is also respectful to other people when you are looking your best."*

Isabel added: *"I don't want to be caught looking like Dracula's sister!"*

But, they certainly are not slaves to their outward appearance. They all seem to get ready in less than no time, and the impression I gained is that they are all so busy with their daily activities that they wouldn't want to waste time unduly on their hair or make-up. I found no obsession with their image at all in my study. Indeed, some women welcome the liberation from worrying about how they look. As Vera commented, *"I don't spend too much time on this as I am in too much of a hurry to get out and about."*

Nevertheless, trips to the hairdresser are frequent, and most of them also enjoy other treats such as massage, manicure, pedicure, facial, electrolysis, eyebrow shaping, reflexology and aromatherapy from time to time. There was widespread recognition that treatments such as these bring benefits such as: *'relaxation', 'feeling refreshed', 'feeling fab', 'making the most of myself', 'great', 'relief of aches and pains', 'feeling more confident in one's appearance', 'ready for action',* and *'happy'.*

They also mentioned using a good moisturiser, eye cream and sunscreen to protect the skin, and light foundation to enhance the complexion. (Favourite products include Nivea, Olay, Avon, Estee Lauder, Mavala, Prescriptives, and 'Mary Kay' in the U.S.A.) But few of the ladies seemed to care much for make-up on a daily basis, especially if it was too heavy and ageing.

What I found interesting about all this is that no one, at any point, said that any of the above was carried out in order to **look younger**. On the contrary, they all seemed quite comfortable as they are and, on looking at their photographs, you can see why. In addition, only one person said that she might consider cosmetic surgery.

Yes, there are laughter lines and some wrinkles, but look at the expression, the radiance, the inner beauty which shines through. See that twinkle and sparkle in their eyes, and sometimes a mischievous glint which is so attractive. There is no doubt that our outward appearance is the truest reflection of what we are feeling inside as we grow older.

So, which would you rather have: a face which is 'Botoxed', lifted and filled in until all you are left with is an immovable pouting mask? Or, a face which shines with inner peace, joy and fulfilment, with laughter lines as evidence of an active, interesting, satisfying life?

Christina Smith

Shelagh Ogilvie Chamberlain

Activity: Bring your face to life

Look at yourself in the mirror.

Now, think of a happy thought inside, pretend you are meeting someone you haven't seen for a long time, and say "Ah, how nice to see you" aloud. Smile as you imagine this encounter.

What do you notice about your face? Does it have more colour now? Can you see how it lights up? Notice how your eyes come to light, how they begin to sparkle. Look at how prominent your cheekbones appear when you smile. When you raise your eyebrows your eyes also come to life.

This exercise is almost as good as having a facelift, but the result is yours for free- it comes from within you. And, don't forget that this is the face that your friends see when you meet for lunch and you are animated and all laughing together, which is another good reason to get out and about as much as possible with uplifting, positive people.

What are some of the other things we can do to make the most of ourselves as we grow older?

Wear colours which enhance your skin and hair colour:

Banish dingy beige and lifeless grey from our wardrobes. Quite simply, as Betty C. says, *"they make you disappear"*. And, why should we fade into the background as we grow older?

Avoid wearing black, dark brown or drab beige next to your face; they drain you of colour and radiance. Cliff at 'Colour Me Beautiful' recommends: *"Avoid black- choose softer tones of dove-grey, rose-brown and navy as your neutrals for skirts and trousers, and wear colour near your face."*

Have fun with scarves and pashminas- they offer an inexpensive way to bring light and colour to the face, especially during our long, dark winter months. Betty S. does this really well- she always wears a scarf in a colour which suits her colouring next to her face. Cliff suggests that softer tones are more flattering as we 'mature'. He says: *"Opt for lilacs, rose-tones, blue-reds, berries, aquas, blues and turquoises."*

For men, these same principles apply. Try a new colour for a tie or scarf- don't be afraid of experimenting.

Consider having a colour consultation with a stylist from 'Colour Me Beautiful' (or similar organisation). They do consultations for both men and women. The money you spend on the consultation will be recouped many times over because you will only buy things which suit your colouring and shape, thus avoiding wastage. As Cliff points out: *"Money doesn't buy style: knowledge does."* Perhaps you could request it for Xmas as a present from a loved one? Alternatively, if a group of you get together for a consultation, it will work out more cheaply, and you can then swap all the clothes which no longer suit your current hair-colour or body shape. (See 'Useful Contacts' to locate your nearest stylist.)

You may have had your colours analysed when you were younger, but, as we age, we may find that our skin <u>tone</u> changes too and, of course, our hair colour may have altered significantly. When a close friend first met her husband, he was already sporting beautiful, silver hair at the age of 41. But, to her horror, his wardrobe was full of brown and khaki clothes which did nothing to enhance his appearance. So, it was out with the dingy browns, and in with cool, sharp colours which totally transformed his image. If your male partner has a problem deciding on his best colours, the book listed in 'Sources' would be a useful starting point.

So...**do a wardrobe audit and:**

KEEP, GIVE AWAY, SWAP, DISCARD or RECYCLE
your entire collection!

Experiment with beauty treatments:

- Take advantage of a free 'make-over' in department stores. Sometimes, just a little change such as a new lip colour or subtle blusher can brighten the face and enhance radiance.
- Similarly, try a facial or other beauty treatment at your local college, where, for a fraction of salon prices, you can have a treatment or massage as a nice treat.
- More and more men are realising the benefits these treatments can bring, so give them a try.

For women, this could include electrolysis for unsightly facial hair and, for everyone, eyebrow shaping to define your eyes. Men should also invest in a hair-trimmer to get rid of ear and nose hair which seems to sprout everywhere as soon as they turn 50. Older men often have eyebrows in which birds could nest, which is very ageing. So, get them shaped, gentlemen!

Seek advice from your hairdresser:

- Next time you visit your hairdresser, ask their advice on hair products and colours which may enhance your current hair condition or colour. They may even provide you with a small sample to try out at home if you are a regular customer.
- It can also be fun to try on wigs in large department stores just to see what you look like in a new style or with a different colour. Some hairdressers can provide computer images of yourself with various hairstyles to see how you look before you go for the chop or a new colour.
- If your hair colour has lightened or faded over the years, experiment with a touch of blusher or a slightly brighter lipstick to ensure your complexion does not look 'faded'. Or, perhaps your hairdresser would recommend some warm (or cool) highlights. Finding the right colour can be difficult and it is best to seek advice.
- Avoid getting into a rut: "Same as usual, Mrs. Smith?" Novelty gives us a lift at any age. So, if your hairdresser cannot come up with some new possibilities which might suit you, it's time to move on.

Buy quality clothes

Betty C., co-owner of a lovely clothes shop in Helmsley, North Yorkshire, has this to say: *"Many people make the mistake of buying lots of cheap clothes. That's fine when you're young, because you would even look good in a plastic bag then. But, when you are older, buy fewer garments made of good material, and make sure they are cut well to enhance your body shape. You can mix and match them, and they will look good for years. In the long term, you actually save money that way."*

Betty always looks elegant and well-groomed and she believes that *"less is more, especially when it comes to jewellery".*

Which items would she avoid? *"Anoraks, fleeces and any shoes with Velcro! I wouldn't be seen dead in those! Also, t-shirts and trousers which reveal wobbly bits and bumps."*

Betty also points out the importance of wearing (and being measured for) the correct bra size, and wearing appropriate undergarments, as the wrong 'undies' can spoil the line of even the most expensive clothes.

In addition:

- Get any dental problems seen to. Not only do tooth problems detract from our appearance, they can also play havoc with our digestion and confidence. Your smile is one of your main assets, so make the most of it.
- Try out any of these suggestions with a friend to make it more fun, and, having another pair of eyes to look at us afresh can be really useful.
- If you wear specs, try out a more 'current' style to give you a boost.
- Cliff at 'Colour Me Beautiful' also recommends that you wear white or rose gold jewellery as it looks so much more expensive than 'yellow' on pink or rosy skin.
- He also recommends covering most of the shoulders, arms and décolletage-use sheer fabrics in warm weather.
- Get decent lighting in your bathroom. What can be worse for morale than lighting that makes us look ten times more tired and washed out than we really are?

It also goes without saying that daily cleansing, toning, weekly exfoliation, daily and nightly moisturising for both men and women will preserve the condition of our skin. Some participants swear by daily use of facial oils which can be useful if your skin is very dry. ('Bio Oil' is affordable and a little goes a long way.) On days when I am very tired, I find the old stand-by, 'Flash Balm' by Clarins, does the trick.

Banish sunbathing, smoking, abuse of alcohol for obvious reasons- we all know what they are by now!!! And, eat well, drink plenty of fluid and do some exercise. All of these bring a glow to the face, and what can be better than a healthy, luminous complexion?

Look around you in the supermarket, and what you will begin to notice is that the people whose trolleys are laden with junk food, cigarettes, lager, sweets and high-fat products have the worst skin, as you would probably expect. (See Chapter 5 to take stock of your diet.)

Activity: Making the most of yourself in this chapter of your life

Scrape your hair back with a neutral hair-band or scarf, and look at yourself in a good, natural light. Don't forget to smile! What are your **best** features? What do you **like** about the way you look **now?** What could you do to highlight and emphasise these features? (e.g. a new scarf to bring out the colour of your eyes, a lipstick, a slick of blusher to accentuate your cheek bones, pluck and shape your eyebrows to emphasise your eyes)

Write down what you **like** about your looks, and also what you can do to enhance them.

Now, do the same appraisal with your hair and your body shape.

Focus ONLY on what you **like** about them. For many of us, this can be a difficult exercise as we focus immediately on what we think is 'wrong' with our looks, so ask a trusted friend, partner or family member for their opinion. Better still, ask several people.

All too often, we only notice the things we don't like about ourselves, and the truth of the matter is that it is highly unlikely that other people see them at all. As I was interviewing the participants, several ladies drew attention to their *"eye bags"* or *"sagging chin".* I can honestly say that I hadn't even noticed as I was so captivated by their sparkle, their twinkling eyes and lively expression.

A note for husbands or lovers

If you are the husband or lover of someone who does not fully appreciate how lovely she is, here is a piece of advice for you: **tell her frequently exactly what it is about her that you find so attractive**. She needs to hear it, and the boost to her self-confidence and self-esteem will bring a blush to her cheeks and a sparkle to her eye. If you are cynical about such things, just think of the money she will save on beauty treatments or face-lifts if a few words from you work as well as the latest products. (Top tip to ladies: leave this page open and highlighted for his benefit!! Even better, tell him what you need to hear- do not assume he will take the hint.)

And, for wives and girlfriends

Men need to be complimented too. Sometimes, it is useful to look at our partner anew to remind ourselves what we found so attractive when we first met him. Then tell him!!

Campaign for more 'mature' models to be featured in the media

Write a letter to at least one company requesting more mature models. Surely they realise that older people buy beauty treatments, clothes and hair products too? If enough of us refuse to purchase their products until they include mature models in advertising, perhaps the message will get through. As the daughter of one of the participants commented: *"They need to wake up to the power of 'the silver dollar'!"*

In conclusion

Above all else, let's resist the temptation to say to friends, *"Oh, how young you look"* or *"You never change".* Instead, say, *"How lovely you look in that dress"* or *"That new colour really suits you- it brings out your lovely brown eyes".*

Celebrate the age we are instead of perpetuating the senseless worship of all things young! As Ann (a former manager with Estee Lauder for 20 years) commented, *"You can't stop the clock."* And, she added just as I was leaving, *"Tell them: don't forget your daily dose of laughter – it's the best beautifier of all!"*

So, always SMILE at yourself in the mirror, and appreciate what you see!

Action planning:

What will you DO with the evidence you have gathered? Hopefully, some of the ideas in this chapter will help you to draw up your action plan. When you do so, remember to add dates against your plans and put these in your diary or calendar. Drawing up a budget so that you can work out costs will also be useful. **Do not feel guilty** about spending some money and time on yourself – you deserve it!

	Action needed	**Date**	**Approximate Cost**
Hair			
Skin care			
Clothes and shoes			
Teeth			
Make-up			
'Treats'			
Other:			

And...**SING!** Facial exercises are useful as they tone up our muscles. However, they can become boring, so **sing** instead. Have you ever noticed how toned opera singers' facial muscles are? In particular, sing songs to the vowels: ae, ee, ah, oh, oo.

Also, try some 'tongue twisters' to tone up. For example, sing these up and down the scale-

'We'll weather the weather whatever the weather...'
'Pretty Penelope, Pretty Penelope...'
'The lips, the teeth, the tip of the tongue...'
'Forty thousand feathers on a thrush...'
'She sells seashells on the sea shore...'

You can do this (practically) anywhere, and you will reap the benefits, not only to your facial muscles, but also your lungs and your posture if you are breathing well and supporting your diaphragm. Notice how your face glows after singing!

4 Keep Moving- How Exercise Can Help, Both Physically and Mentally

What is your attitude towards exercise? Do you enjoy it or loathe it? Which types of exercise do you currently participate in? What benefits do you feel you derive from them? Which incentives would encourage you to exercise more?

Hopefully, this chapter will inspire and motivate you to find an exercise plan which suits you and your personality. I must confess that I have never been an exercise fanatic, but, after researching this chapter, I realised that I had to 'up my game'. After all, if the 70 to 88 year-old participants in my research could do all these things (see below), what excuse could I possibly have for taking the bus into town when I could walk, or catching the lift from the beach to the top of the Esplanade in Scarborough? Shame, I discovered, can provide a powerful incentive to do more!!!

What the participants do and why:

I was astonished and impressed by the wide variety of exercise in which the participants engage on a regular basis.

These included: walking (including dog-walking), hiking, rambling (up to 8 miles!), hill-walking, yoga, gardening, digging, swimming, exercise classes, water aerobics, gym, rowing machine, housework, short tennis, cycling, DVD programmes, emulsioning ceilings, 'Health Rider', dancing, including ballroom dancing, golf, step aerobics and 'Fitness League'. Phew!!

The benefits they reported are-

Physical: Maureen, who is always 'on the move', comments that exercise *"Improves mobility, tones up my muscles, promotes energy and stimulates the circulation."* Ann stressed the need for self-discipline, and she found that her recovery following knee surgery was much better than those who did not follow the recommended exercise programme.

These points were echoed by others in the group, and many mentioned the value of keeping supple through exercise. Sue S. highlighted the extra energy she derives from exercise, and this seemed to be another important motivator amongst the role models.

Maureen Robinson

In addition, with no prompting from me, they all commented on the other benefits they derive from exercise, including:

Cognitive: Most of the participants find that exercise also helps them to feel more alert, and, as D. said, *"Fitter in mind as well as body."* This is certainly borne out by research which we will review presently.

Social: Vera finds, *"When I exercise I feel more cheerful, especially when exercising in the company of others."*

Jessie joined the 'Ramblers' Association' when she retired and finds the company of others provides fun and companionship when out walking. She added that, when you join a group, you meet new people with whom you can also have a coffee and chat. For Betty C., getting out and about leads to *"Meeting interesting people"* and she enjoys a glass of champagne afterwards! Now that sounds like a good incentive.

Vera Cameron

Emotional: Several participants noted that exercise aids relaxation and lowers stress levels. For example, Betty S. said, *"It calms your thoughts, and you are less likely to dwell on the negative side of things."* She went on to say, *"It makes you glad to be alive."* In addition, Jessie noted that, *"I find an increased ability to cope with problems when they crop up."*

I hope these accounts have kindled your interest in expanding your exercise programme.

Jessie also made the most important point that it is vital to focus on what one **can do and enjoy** rather than competing against others or worrying about what you used to be able to do. She suggests that you set your own goals, which is a point we will return to presently. (Having said that, she then went on to tell me that she '*only*' manages to hill-walk up to 1,000 feet... swim 34 lengths... and walk for 8 miles now that she is 79!)

Maybe you are already thinking of some goals for your action plan?

But, what about exercise for those who are less mobile, perhaps following a stroke, operation or for other reasons?

Perhaps 'Extend' can help

I was invited to attend an exercise class which is organised as part of a national project called 'Extend'. The class is aimed at the over 60's and anyone with physical disabilities who might find a typical exercise class difficult to access.

The lovely tutor, Ketyn Jepson, explained to me that most of the class is based on chair-based exercise to music, and the emphasis is on what one can do comfortably and safely. So, I went along with an open mind, and found I had the best fun I have ever had in any exercise class. The exercises are all done to really upbeat music and each part of the body is targeted in turn (including pelvic floor exercises). Throughout, Ketyn encouraged everyone to have a go, but stop if anything felt uncomfortable.

I loved every minute of it and found the exercises really focused my concentration as well as gently addressing all the muscles. What I also observed was how much brighter everyone seemed at the end of the class. I was pleasantly surprised at how much active exercise can be performed whilst seated.

Classes like these are available all round the U.K., so do consider popping along to have a go. All Extend tutors are highly trained, the class only costs a few pounds to attend (at time of writing) and you are certain to enjoy it. In addition, you may make some new friends over a cup of tea after the class. (See 'Contacts' at the end of the book for further details of these classes, and also a DVD of chair based exercises which would be useful for those who are unable to attend a class.)

Still not convinced? Here are a few findings from published research:

One of the key factors cited in studies of long-living communities and individuals is: 'exercising regularly but not excessively'.

But what exactly does this mean in practice? My interpretation of 'regularly' and 'excessively' may differ widely from yours, and this is one of the frustrations I encountered when analysing the research in this area. It appears I am not alone in feeling this way. Barbara Strauch (2010) was told by scientists she interviewed that they are still unsure exactly how much exercise is recommendable for the brain.

Aim for a mile

However, more helpfully, the neuroscientist Art Kramer has discovered that over 60's who spent approximately an hour walking around a gym three times a week at a very achievable pace of three miles an hour increased their brain volume appreciably. Both the grey and white matter increased. (Cited in Strauch, 2010)

In another of Art Kramer's studies, a group of 124 unfit over-60's walked for 45 minutes three times a week at a pace of 17.7 minutes per mile. The results revealed that they made important gains in complex tasks which involved: focusing, task switching, rapidly answering questions, and other frontal-lobe challenges. The participants who performed best were those who managed to walk a mile in 16 minutes.

I find these results very encouraging because they are within the reach of many of us, and they provide us with something really concrete and specific to set as one of our goals. It is also fairly easy to integrate this goal within our daily lives. So, for those who may feel daunted by the very idea of an 'exercise programme', these results offer a very good starting point. Using a pedometer will help you to monitor how far you have walked, and you can then increase your targets as you gain more stamina.

Kramer's work also confirms what many of my participants say about the benefits of exercise- it does help to keep our brains sharp!

Maintain your balance

In Robert Dilts' (1992) study of good elderly role models, one of his discoveries was the importance of being symmetrical in gestures and movements. As a devotee of T'ai Chi, I found this of great interest as, in the practice of T'ai Chi, each movement is replicated exactly on either side. This may be of particular interest to anyone suffering from balance problems caused by inner ear conditions such as Meniere's Disease which can wreak havoc with balance as the condition progresses. When I was diagnosed with this condition many years ago, I embarked on a series of balance retraining exercises advocated by the Meniere's Society. (Please see the address under 'Contacts'.) These are clearly explained in one of their booklets. The Meniere's Society's research demonstrates that balance exercises can benefit many people who suffer from vertigo or dizziness. I am convinced that my balance is much better than it used to be (and certainly no worse) as a result of combining daily T'ai Chi with balance exercises.

This becomes particularly relevant as we grow older as so many unfortunate falls are attributable to loss of balance. Ketyn Jepson from Age U.K. (Scarborough and District) commented that: *"Around 30 per cent of people over 65, and 50 per cent of over 80s fall each year."* The good thing about rebalancing exercises and learning T'ai Chi (or Yoga or Pilates) is that you can build them up at any age, at your own pace, and set your own goals. They also provide a very good way of focusing the mind, relaxing, and breathing correctly, which you can continue to do (adapted to your changing circumstances) for as long as you live.

Other benefits

Building muscle is also associated with longevity. Professor Peter Katzmarzyk at Pennington Biomedical Research Centre, Louisiana, has discovered that those people with more muscle are more likely to live longer. So, let's all get pumping!

In addition, it is well-documented that weight-bearing exercise helps to protect our bones from the debilitating effects of osteoporosis. This can include: brisk walking, keep-fit classes, jogging, dancing, etc, which enable your feet and legs to support your weight. (Make sure you wear supportive footwear.)

Fred Gage, a prominent researcher in the field of neuroscience, recommends that we should exercise at something for at least 30 minute a day to help our brain stay in good shape. (Cited in Strauch, 2010) In chapter 7, we will discover more about how exercise can help to keep the brain active. The main point from the research I reviewed (too extensive to include here) is that lethargy and immobility provide our bodies and our brains with no benefits at all, so... get moving!!

Planning Your New Scenario

It's never too late to embark on exercise or to find something that works for you!

As Howard Friedman and Leslie Martin (2011) discovered in their Longevity Project, those who start active and stay active tend to remain healthy, **but** so do those who start out less active and then *increase and maintain their level of activity.* Once again, persistence and prudence pay dividends. So, don't despair; even if you have never exercised much, it's not too late to start.

The key is to be realistic: all too many diet and exercise programmes fail because people start off with great intentions but find it impossible to maintain the original impetus, so they 'fall off the saddle' and give up.

If you plan your goals using the SMART formula below, then you are much more likely to make lasting improvements to your exercise schedule. The aim is to find some form of exercise which can become part of your lifestyle for as long as possible.

So, your goal must be:

Specific – (e.g. I am going to buy a rowing machine)

Measurable – (e.g. I will use it every second day, starting with 5 minutes on setting 2, and increasing both time and setting as I gain strength and stamina)

Accountable – (e.g. I will share my goals with my friend, Sue, so we can encourage each other in our exercise programmes)

Realistic – (e.g. I know I can do this as it will fit in with my everyday activities)

Time bound – (e.g. I will order it at the week-end and start using it as soon as it arrives. I will mark my progress on my calendar to give myself a visual reminder. By Xmas, I will be able to row for 15 minutes on setting 3.)

But, which goals will be right for you?

We are all different, and it is really important to find various **types** of exercise which you enjoy and to formulate your goals in a way which is right for **YOU**, otherwise it is highly unlikely that you will stay with them long enough to gain any benefit.

So, what would **suit you**, and what do you **need?**

Tick your preferences:

- I prefer indoor/ outdoor exercise
- I like to exercise alone/ in a group/ with a 'buddy'
- I like scheduled/ unscheduled exercise
- I want/ don't want to be supervised (e.g. in a gym, class or with a trainer)
- I like/ don't like to use special equipment
- I prefer competitive/ non-competitive exercise
- I want to focus on stamina/ strength/ balance/ all of these
- I prefer dance-type exercise
- I like slow/ fast exercise
- I would like/ wouldn't like to work with weights
- I need a 'carrot'/ 'stick' to keep me motivated
- Other:

For example, I really hate swimming or any form of water-based activity. Neither am I into competitive sport of any kind. But, I do like the outdoors and walking, and I love moving to music. However, scheduled classes would not suit me because of my varied work schedule. I know that I do have the self-discipline to use equipment at home. Also, as I sometimes find it hard to slow down and relax, it is good to combine fast exercise with some slow-down activity.

How about you? What are your likes and dislikes?

By being attuned to **your** needs and what suits you, you will gain much more from your choices and be more likely to commit long-term to them.

In my case, I find a combination of T'ai Chi (with and without music), stretching, walking briskly, and using a rowing machine at home seem to work well within my daily routine.

Remember that a **varied programme** is best as it enables you to use different muscles, work on stamina and balance as well as strength, and, if possible, build in exercise which helps you to relax too.

Write down overleaf any other considerations which you need to include in your plan such as costs, time, medical factors, etc. **If you are unsure about medical considerations, check with your G.P. or Consultant before you embark on any exercise programme.**

(If you plan to join an Extend class, you will have to complete a 'Safe to Exercise' questionnaire before you begin.)

Then write your SMART goals:

Specific

Measurable

Accountable

Realistic

Time bound

Build up gradually, and modify your goals as you achieve them

Interviewing the participants opened my eyes to what is possible. If I am honest, I think that I was erring on the side of 'laziness' before I started doing my research.

I have found that just increasing the distance I walk every day, staying on the rowing machine a little longer and walking up the cliffs in Scarborough instead of taking the lift have increased my stamina and also provided a sense of achievement. Sometimes, small changes bring real benefits. Even things such as being more active around the house and garden or in town can make a difference (as many of the participants demonstrate).

For example:

- Walking around during a long phone call
- Really getting stuck into the housework
- Going up the stairs slightly faster
- Using the stairs when shopping instead of the lift or escalator
- Doing your tummy or bottom clenches when you are washing up
- Getting up and having a good stretch during the TV adverts
- Walking a bit more quickly and swinging your arms more
- 'Conducting' to your favourite music
- Gardening with a bit more vigour

What realistic, small changes could you build into your daily life which would make a difference to you, both physically and mentally? Plan some below:

Be mindful, and monitor what helps or hinders you

Ellen Langer (2010) advocates the practice of mindfulness, especially in being attuned to our bodies. Notice even the small changes, both mentally and physically. Be especially vigilant for any adverse effects after exercise and modify your programme accordingly. Celebrate your achievements and your progress, however small the steps forward. Make a daily note of what you have achieved and how you feel.

Robert Dilts (1992) found that the 'role models' in his research on ageing well did more of what they found worked for them and helped them to achieve their goals, and they relinquished what they found unhelpful. There is no point in ploughing on with a programme which does not suit you, either physically or mentally. There are plenty of alternatives, so explore those instead.

As I have said before, we are all different, so *'to thine own self be true.'*

Pre-empt and plan strategies for possible setbacks

Gerard Egan (1990) says the two most common reasons for failing to achieve our goals are **'entropy'** and **'inertia.'**

Entropy is what happens when we start off any programme with great enthusiasm, and for whatever reason, it tails off. Sometimes this is referred to as 'the ubiquitous decay curve.'

Inertia is what stops us from getting started at all!

By being aware of these risks and planning for them, we are much more likely to succeed. A useful model to use is called 'force field analysis' which was first developed by Kurt Lewin way back in 1947. I find it just as relevant and useful today. What Kurt Lewin explains is that, when we are trying to effect changes in our lives, there may be forces which will help us to achieve our goals, and forces which may get in our way. In order to be successful, the forces in our favour must outweigh the forces against us.

To illustrate how it works, I will use my own example of planning to increase my walking and to walk (or rather climb!) home from the beach instead of taking the lift.

On the chart opposite, I have indicated the possible factors which may help me on the left, and those which may obstruct me on the right.

Helping me	Hindering me
→	←
I love the scenery around Scarborough	I hate walking in the wind and rain
→	←
I can visualise myself getting fitter	I can be quite lazy sometimes
→	
I will save some money	
→	
I really want to stay slim and trim	

As you can see in my example, the forces 'for' outweigh the forces 'against' my chances of success. I have also coloured the really important factors in green to remind me to focus my mind and attention on those. You could draw the arrows under the most important factors bigger and bolder to emphasise their potential strength.

Create your own Force Field Analysis below:

Helping me	Hindering me
→	←

But, what about the rainy, windy days when the bus seems much more attractive? And those days when energy seems to desert me (or you) and we just can't be bothered?

Different incentives work for different people, but try some of these suggestions:

- **Visualise** yourself <u>already</u> achieving your goals. Creating a strong visual image of your success will reinforce your motivation and determination.
- **Reward yourself** with a treat which you work towards when you stick with your plan over a period of time of your own choosing. In my case, having quite a short focus when it comes to exercise, a fortnight is long enough.
- **Saving** money towards a treat can also be useful. So, each time you do your exercise programme, or you walk instead of taking the bus, put (let's say) 50p in a jar, and treat yourself after a few months.
- **Team up with a buddy** who will encourage, cajole and support you as you do the same for him or her.
- **Join a club or group** of like-minded individuals who are already succeeding. Ask them what <u>their</u> strategies are. How do they keep going even when they don't feel like exercising? When I asked Jessie this question, she told me, *"Och, I just say to myself 'I'll enjoy it when I get there', and I find that I do."*
- Gerard Egan (1990) suggests: 'Imagine you are now at zero. What would it take to get to one?' This is useful if getting started is your main challenge.
- Who are your **role models?** Try to imagine (or ask them!) how they motivate themselves? What do they do to get moving? Thinking like a winner is a tried and tested technique in all physical training, so try it for yourself.
- **Do ten... and then see**. My friend, Caroline Fanshawe, suggests that you do ten lengths, minutes, exercises, whatever, and then see. The chances are that you will want to do more, but, even if you do not, at least you have done <u>some</u> exercise.
- Make a note below of the **motivational techniques** you know of and can apply to your programme:

In addition, stick around those **people** who are positive and encouraging. Make a note of who they are below, and try to spend more time with them. Howard Friedman and Leslie Martin (2011) found that associating with people who want to be active and healthy is a key factor in establishing long-lasting, beneficial changes in our lives, so choose your company wisely.

What I need – Someone to:	**Who might support me?**	**Who to avoid?** (i.e. discouraging types or people who are uninterested in healthy habits)
Encourage me		
Pass on their skills and knowledge		
'Chivvy' me along		
Exercise with		
Other –		

And, what of the **'buts'?**

"But I can't do any of that because I'm... arthritic, too busy, have no energy, can't afford it, the weather is bad, I feel cold today, I have a sore throat, etc., etc."

As Ketyn Jepson's group at 'Extend' have discovered, focus on what you CAN DO, however small it seems, and you will feel better in body, mind and spirit. The choice is yours- keep moving and reap the benefits, or become a TV watching, couch potato and reduce your life expectancy- brutal, I know, but backed up by sound research in a recent report from the British Journal of Sports Medicine. It's time to be rid of excuses. Write them down, rip them up and throw them where they belong- in your dustbin. This is your life, and you need to make the most of it. **Start moving now, today.**

A final thought... Did you know that Helen Mirren (aged 66) was recently voted 'Los Angeles Fitness Body of the Year'? She beat Elle MacPherson, Kelly Brook, Cheryl Cole and Jennifer Lo!

Above all, remember that, as Gerard Egan (1990) reminds us, even if we have a lapse in our programme, this need not spell disaster and feeling that all is lost. We all have our 'off days'. So, get back into your programme as soon as you can and keep focusing on what you **are** achieving: don't beat yourself up if this seems small. Every step counts.

And...**SING!!!** As the 8,000 participants in 'Rock Choirs' are discovering, singing, when combined with some movement, is a gentle form of aerobic exercise which increases stamina, makes us breathe more deeply, increases the heart rate, improves our posture and gives us extra energy and vitality. It also reduces stress levels and helps us to sleep better. At time of writing (August, 2011), the most senior member of Rock Choir was 88! So, put on your favourite CD and sing and dance your heart out.

(See 'Useful Contacts' to locate your nearest Rock Choir.)

5 Have a Little Bit of What You Fancy…

Before you start reading this chapter, take a few minutes to review your answers to the questions below when you completed your Baseline Questionnaire (Appendix 1):

- **How would you sum up your approach to eating and drinking?**

- **Are you happy with your weight?**

Then, consider:

- **If you are not happy with your weight, why is that? What would you like to do about it?**

- **What do you think are your current strengths and targets in relation to your diet and drinking habits?**

(Later in the chapter, we will return to these questions in more depth.)

These were some of the questions I asked the role models. In this chapter, we will analyse their responses, then we will examine some other research findings before going on to provide you with tools and strategies to enable you to devise a method of eating and drinking which works for you. We are all different, and there is no one method which will 'guarantee' your health for the foreseeable future. Nothing comes with a warranty: all we can do is to keep up to date with research, learn from good role models, and do the best we can to eat and drink as healthily as possible.

Do consult your G.P. or Clinician before changing your diet radically. As I am not a doctor, I am not going to offer advice or diet sheets: this chapter is about taking informed responsibility for your own health. This approach puts you firmly in 'the driving seat'.

The participants' approach to eating and drinking was varied, as one would expect, but here are the general points and the things they seem to have in common:

a) Their diet is mainly balanced and they all cook for themselves, using raw ingredients, as far as possible, rather than 'junk food', ready made meals, or 'take-aways'.

b) Although some of them said they might like to 'drop a few pounds', none of them can be described as clinically obese. They certainly are not obsessing about losing weight, and, as Susan laughingly said: *"If I lose weight, my wrinkles might show"*.

c) None of them are smokers (although a few had 'dabbled' socially when they were much younger and it was fashionable to smoke).

d) None of them were currently 'on a diet' to lose weight, and most said they enjoyed their food but, in Kate's words, ***"I do not live to eat"***. Similarly, Dorothy told me that she *"is not a food fanatic"*. She could happily live without food because it would free up time to do other interesting things.

Kate Owens

e) Their drinking habits are very moderate. Some are teetotal, but most enjoy a little 'tipple' on social occasions, and a few have a regular glass of wine with their meals.

f) There was very wide variation with regards to taking vitamin supplements. Some are dedicated to specific vitamins and supplements; others cannot see the point of it all, and they prefer to focus on consuming a healthy diet.

g) They all eat fruit and vegetables every day.

h) Many mentioned the wartime diet and how healthy people were then because they grew their own vegetables, and sweets, chocolate and sugar were all rationed. Kate, for example, commented that *"the habits learned during the war are maybe paying off now"*.

i) They do not deprive themselves of 'treats', but the general motto is 'a little of what you fancy does you good.' In other words, their eating is not out of control. One lady told me that, when her friends come round for coffee, they each bring a small cake (i.e. individual portion) so that they can all enjoy one each *"without overdoing it"*.

j) They are all very aware of making healthy choices, but try to do so without becoming 'slaves' to any regimen.

k) Most of them drink tea and/or coffee every day. (Rusty looks forward to her daily treat of *"one delicious latté"*!)

l) They try to cut down on salt, sugar and high fat in their diet. (Some with more success than others, it has to be said.)

I also asked the participants to keep a food diary for three days so that I could gain a closer insight into their daily eating habits. I was impressed by the **variety** in their diets, the amount of **fruit and vegetables** consumed and the healthy **balance** achieved on a daily basis. No wonder they are all so lively, energetic and mentally alert! It is an old cliché, but so true: '*we are what we eat.*' Here is the evidence, but, of course, this is a very small-scale study. So, what have researchers from larger projects discovered which might be useful to us?

A confusing, often contradictory, picture

If you (like me) are hoping to read some straightforward guidelines which will enable you to devise an optimum action plan, then, I am sorry to say, there are none. I found the published research I reviewed contradictory, sometimes vague and often sponsored by pharmaceutical companies who have a vested interest in seducing us into buying their vitamin supplements.

Let's take the craze for blueberries as an example. In practically every newspaper recently we are told that they are the latest discovery in keeping our brains healthy, but, what I want to know is: how many should I take; is it best to cook them first; should they be eaten at one go or regularly throughout the day, etc.

Similarly, most of us (unless we have been on an extended vacation on Mars) know that Omega 3 is good for us, but, once again, the advice on how much to take, in what form- pills, capsules or 'real' food, and so on, is widely contradictory. As Mark Moss (a neuroscientist at Boston University) told Barbara Strauch (2010), every year we seem to be given a new message or dictum.

Ellen Langer (2010) likens this to a scene in Woody Allen's movie, *'Sleeper'* where the principal character awakens after a long sleep to find that everything that used to be good for him is now considered bad, and vice versa.

Studies of role models

However, research involving good role models does throw some light on the picture. For example, Robert Dilts' (1992) summary of studies of long-living, active adults identifies that they:

- drink moderately (1 or 2 alcoholic drinks a day)
- do not smoke
- eat a low fat, low sugar, low calorie diet, and
- are not overweight.

This appears to concur with the findings from my research study.

Likewise, many researchers have been fascinated by the people of Okinawa (sometimes referred to as 'the island of long life') who frequently live active, vital lives to the age of 100 and more. Their diet mainly consists of:

- fish
- soya
- algae (rich in iron and calcium)
- rice
- green tea.

What is also noteworthy is that they tend to eat **slowly**, savouring each mouthful, and they stop eating when they feel 80% full. They don't eat sweet foods or pastries, and it is interesting that those who migrate to other places and adopt a different diet have a reduced life span. This strongly supports the idea that it is the diet and lifestyle which are the key factors rather than genetic variables.

Lewis Wolpert (2011) adds that the calorie consumption of those living in Okinawa is also 20 per cent less than the Japanese average. Death rates for heart disease, strokes and cancer are around two thirds that for Japan as a whole. The death rate for 60 year-olds is approximately half that of Japan's national average.

However, these figures may not be attributable to diet alone. Residents of Okinawa also pursue a lifestyle based on spiritual practices such as meditation, prayer, T'ai Chi, and mindfulness. Moreover, they also have a robust, optimistic outlook on life. In addition, they eat their meals in a leisurely, relaxed way without distractions such as television. Their lifestyle revolves around mutual cooperation and being part of the wider society. I find it difficult to separate the key factors responsible for their longevity as they appear to be inextricably linked together.

Lewis Wolpert reports that this is particularly true of exercise. In his book, *'You're looking well!'* (2011), he reviews a study of people in New York with an average age of 77. They all consumed a Mediterranean-style diet, rich in fruit, vegetables, fish, cereal and pulses, and low in meat. But, what the researchers found was that the group **who also exercised** had a 60 per cent reduced risk of developing dementia.

Those who did not exercise showed a 40 per cent reduction. Thus, it appears that a **combination** of healthy diet and exercise is significant.

Here are some other findings which I think may be of value to you in making informed decisions about your health:

Obesity, type 2 diabetes and dementia

Researchers in Sweden, led by Dr. Weili Xu at the Karolinska Institutet, Stockholm, have found that controlling your weight in middle age can reduce your risk of suffering from dementia. In an extensive study of the medical records of over 8,500 twins over a period of 30 years, researchers concluded that people who were overweight or obese in mid-life had an 80% higher risk of developing dementia.

An earlier study in Finland (2005) focused on 1,449 randomly selected participants. Researchers monitored their records at the age of 51 and then again when they were 72. Those who suffered from mid-life obesity doubled their risk for dementia, and those who had been obese in mid-life **and** also suffered from high blood pressure **and** high levels of cholesterol (i.e. all three risk factors) were six times more likely to experience dementia. (Reported in Strauch, 2010)

Similarly, a number of studies have found that people who suffer from type 2 diabetes are more likely to develop Alzheimer's.

Barbara Strauch concludes that obesity in middle age does us no favours. This strikes me as being something of an understatement.

The Mediterranean Diet and B vitamins

David Smith and his team of researchers at Oxford University (the Oxford Project to Investigate Memory and Ageing- 'OPTIMA') followed 3,000 people for four years and found that those who had the highest intake of olive oil, nuts, fish, tomatoes, poultry, vegetables, fruits and dark leafy vegetables were less likely to succumb to Alzheimer's. This was particularly the case in those who had a lower intake of high-fat dairy and red meat.

His team also discovered that low levels of vitamin B12 were associated with brain shrinkage. Professor Smith believes that anyone over the age of 40 should make sure they consume adequate daily amounts of folate, B6 and B12. He points out that these B vitamins help to control levels of homocysteine in the blood, high levels of which can accelerate brain shrinkage. (Do discuss this with your G.P. before self-medicating, however.)

Tracy Lawson (2011) spent a year in the 'Village of Eternity', Campodimele, in Italy, to discover the secrets of the villagers' longevity and active, healthy lifestyles. Not surprisingly, their diet conforms to the 'Mediterranean diet' described above, and they only eat food in season, grown without chemicals. But, as researchers have found in other studies, the villagers also follow a very stress-free lifestyle; they build exercise into their everyday routines of tending the fields and cycling or walking up into the hillsides; they are sociable, and their schedules are attuned to the seasons and rhythms of nature. They also sleep a good eight hours every night.

So, it would appear that a healthy diet is necessary, but not sufficient, if we want to remain lively and well in our old age.

Why is everyone talking about antioxidants?

You may be wondering why there is so much fuss about eating blueberries and foods which are rich in antioxidants, such as vitamins C and E, and beta-carotene. Barbara Strauch (2010) explains that, when we grow older, antioxidants (our 'defence system') cannot keep apace of free radicals (resulting from exposure to pollution, radiation, and ultra-violet light), and more of our brain cells can be damaged which can accelerate the ageing process. In addition, other writers point out that wider cellular damage throughout our bodies can occur if damage from free radicals occurs. This can cause cells to function poorly or even die off.

So, to combat the potential damage caused by free radicals, researchers believe we need to consume plenty of colourful fruits which are rich in antioxidants such as red peppers, tomatoes, oranges, blackberries, red grapes, kiwi fruit, etc, and vegetables such as kale, spinach and broccoli.

The more intensely colourful your diet, the better, is the current advice on offer. But, much more research, including clinical trials, must be carried out to provide precise guidelines for us to follow.

So – what do you think?

This is probably a good point to stop and reflect on the findings discussed so far.

Are you feeling confused, reassured, bored, uplifted, smug...?

A good way forward may be to consider good role models you know who have lived to a healthy, lively, alert old age. What are their eating, drinking and lifestyle habits? Do some research- they will probably love to be asked.

Of course, there is always the exception to the rule. People are fond of citing their 'Auntie Alice' who lived to be 95, smoked like a chimney, imbibed half a bottle of whisky every day and lived on a diet of fish and chips.

But, seriously, what might be some of the **key points** emerging from these studies which could help you in your quest to enjoy good health in your golden years? What might you do differently? Quite clearly, we need to start thinking about this long before we reach old age. But, thinking alone is unlikely to make any difference: **action** is required.

Noteworthy points to consider:

What works for YOU?

In order to make effective decisions, why not record what you eat and drink over a three day period- be totally honest! (The chart in Appendix 2 can be photocopied.)

In addition, make a note of:

- **Where** you were eating. At your desk? In the car? While watching T.V.? At the table with your family? Secretly?
- **How** you were eating. Slowly and savouring each mouthful? At speed because you were ravenous? Gobbling it down because it was something like chocolate or cake and you felt guilty? Mindlessly while you were doing something else?
- **When** are you eating? At regular mealtimes? Having a little, often, during the day? Not eating all day and then having a heavy meal late at night? Binging when you feel upset?
- **Why** were you eating or drinking? Was it for comfort or to alleviate stress? Were you genuinely hungry? Were you bored? Is it a love substitute?
- **How** did you feel **afterwards?** 80% full like the centenarians in Okinawa? Bloated and queasy? Still hungry? Guilty?

Ellen Langer advises that, as adults, we know our own bodies better than any doctor can. However, by becoming more mindful and aware of even subtle changes in our bodies, we can get to know what works and does not work for us as individuals. That is why record keeping can be useful. In addition, it will highlight the emotional reasons why our dietary and drinking habits may need to be addressed.

What I am suggesting is that we all try to re-establish what Julian Rotter (1966) defined as our *'internal locus of control'*. What he found in his research was that people who had a stronger sense of internal control are much more likely to <u>do</u> something to help themselves than those whose locus of control is external. By putting ourselves back 'in control', we can take more adult responsibility for our health and well-being.

One of the problems of following diet sheets and lists of 'allowed foods' and 'sinful' foods is that we become like hapless children bowing to the externally imposed rules of some dominant 'expert'. (And, of course, rules are 'meant to be broken'!)

Instead, monitor your reactions and responses to your current eating and drinking schedules and routines.

Then, as the intelligent adult that you are, you can decide what the strengths and 'targets' are. Retain what is good for you, doing you good and making you feel good, both physically and emotionally. And, tweak, chuck out, change anything that is not contributing to your sense of well-being. (Use the chart in Appendix 2 to help you plan what to do.)

RETAIN	TWEAK	STOP!

If you can incorporate some of the healthy practices discussed in this chapter, so much the better. Ellen Langer (2010, p.186) makes a very useful distinction between **'staying healthy'** and **'being made well by the medical profession'** which is an important point for us all to consider. By focusing on staying healthy, we take more responsibility for our well-being, and this will encourage us all to use mindfulness to assess how efficient (or inefficient) our lifestyles are in keeping us in good health.

So, small, realistic, achievable steps today can make a lasting difference in the future. Modify just one thing at a time so that you can monitor the outcomes, and get to know and respect your own unique body. Treat it well if you want to feel well. Professor Friedman from the Longevity Project (2011) points out that it is never too late to choose a healthier path. This is good news for us all.

Key aspects to notice both before and after you modify your habits:

- **Digestion/ indigestion** – what agrees with you and what doesn't?
- **Bowel regularity and amounts.** (Yes, you do need to have a look!) Be particularly vigilant if any blood is observed in the stools and/or changes in bowel habits.
- **Mood** (especially stability versus mood swings).
- **Energy levels** – are they constant? Do they fluctuate (i.e. spikes and troughs)?
- **Does eating breakfast make a difference? Which breakfast works best for you?** (Note well that all the respondents in my study who submitted three-day menus eat a well-balanced breakfast.)
- **Strength and stamina** – are you full of beans, or feeling tired and listless? Do you ever feel weak or faint after eating certain foods?
- **Stress levels**
- **Sleep patterns**
- **Weight gain or loss**
- **Alertness, concentration**
- **Memory**
- **Other** –

Make sure you **do more** of what is helping and **reduce** what is hindering you in your quest to stay healthy as Professor Friedman suggests. And, of course, if you have concerns, make an appointment to see your G.P.. S/he will find the records you have kept very useful.

The section at the end of the previous chapter on exercise will help you to stay focused on your action plan and your goals, so incorporate those strategies too. Remember that you may have good and bad days, but, as Winston Churchill said:

'Success is maintaining your enthusiasm between failures.'

And, it's official- a little of what you fancy does you good!

Here's the good news – researchers working in the OPTIMA project have found that consuming the following daily can **improve brain cognition:**

- a little piece of <u>dark</u> chocolate (aim for 70-80% cocoa to gain maximum benefits from the flavanoid content)
- half a glass of red wine, and
- unlimited amounts of tea.

Dark chocolate also stimulates the production of endorphins- the 'feel-good' hormones- and it contains anti-oxidants.

In addition, French researchers have discovered that women who drink three cups of coffee a day are 30% less likely to suffer memory loss than non-coffee drinkers. In 80 year-olds, the figure was an impressive 70%. So, carry on with the daily lattés, Rusty!

Indeed, according to research by neuroscientist, Dr. Jack Lewis, which has been widely reported in the press recently, resisting temptation can make us feel angry, dissatisfied and deprived. Conversely, he says that we need to learn to enjoy a little treat without feeling guilty. (But, before you get too excited, note well that this particular research was funded by 'Gu Puds'. As I warned before in this chapter, companies have a vested interest in carrying out research which lures us into buying their products, so always scrutinise the research sponsors!!!)

Of course, the key word is ***'little'.*** What I observe in my friends who constantly battle with their weight is a tendency to deprive themselves of things such as chocolate and cakes while they are on (yet another) diet, and then they binge on the 'forbidden fruits', feel they have failed and abandon the diet. They also tell me that they gobble down these foods as quickly as possible (often alone and in secret) without even taking time to enjoy the taste.

Contrast this with the role models and you find that they really enjoy a small piece of chocolate, a nice home-made cake, a latte or a chilled glass of champagne without feeling guilty. They also like to take their time to relax and savour the moment slowly in the company of good friends.

So, how can you learn to do the same?

Hopefully, keeping a record of what, where, when, how and why you eat and drink will help you to identify good patterns of behaviour which, of course, you will aim to retain.

But, if you uncover the kinds of dysfunctional patterns which include binging, feeling guilty, yo-yo weight gain and loss, self-induced vomiting or eating far too little, seek help from a therapist who has specialist knowledge of eating disorders. Don't battle with this problem on your own for years. Get to the root **causes** of **why** you eat or drink in this way, and then do the hard work of breaking the cycle. (See 'Contacts' for details of organisations which can help.)

Keep your sights on the goal ahead which will be to eat and drink healthily thus avoiding many problems which are associated with obesity and high alcohol consumption when you are older, and you will be able to enjoy a little treat now and again.

Finally...

Small steps can make a long-term, significant difference. Ellen Langer (2011) points out that trying to do something huge such as losing fifty pounds might seem totally impossible. But, most of us can cope with the real possibility of losing just one ounce.

What is **your** '*ounce*'- that one small step- which can make a lasting difference to your health?

And...**SING!!!!** Every time you are tempted to comfort eat, binge on ice-cream, or consume another glass of wine, distract yourself by singing. By the time you finish, you will be feeling so much better about yourself that the moment of temptation will be gone.

6 Cultivate Good Relationships and an Uplifting Social Life

According to a recent survey conducted by 'Elderly Parents' (an organisation set up to provide support and advice for people caring for older parents), fear of being alone becomes a key source of anxiety as we grow older. 'Elderly Parents' discovered that half the respondents feared isolation and lack of contact with friends and relatives in their old age.

Without exception, the participants in my research cited good relationships as a key factor in their feeling of well-being and zest for life. This is a crucial issue for many of us, especially those who live alone, either through choice or because of circumstances. Many of us also live at considerable distance from family and, if we are new to a place, may not have a network of people we feel close to.

In this chapter, we will examine our current situation and consider ways in which we might ensure that we maximise the benefits which socialising and close relationships offer, especially as we grow older. For what could be worse than going for weeks on end without having a meaningful conversation with anyone?

Let's begin with a key question: Are you nice to be around?

When I met with the participants, I was struck by how easy they were to be with, and how much I enjoyed their company. There was an absence of self-pity, even in the face of illness or caring for a loved one. In Marie de Hennezel's book (2011), she discusses some of the attributes and social skills which seem to attract others to our company. I found these resonated closely with what I observed in the participants and included:

- Simply being nice
- A pleasant tone of voice, including on the telephone

- Never complaining
- Taking an interest in others
- Looking at life with gratitude for what we have
- Leaving behind our egocentricity, and entering the other person's world
- Smiling
- Being receptive
- Tolerance
- Being open-minded
- Having a good sense of humour
- Having a generosity of self
- Expecting nothing from others, but expressing sincere thankfulness for what is offered

When I think of my favourite friends and relatives, the ones whose company I seek out, simply because I want to be with them (not through a sense of 'duty'), are those who display all the above qualities (and then some!!).

Tim Drake and Chris Middleton (2009) make an interesting distinction between ***'radiators'*** and ***'drains'***. Betty C. is a prime example of a 'radiator'- you just feel better after being in her company because she brings joy and warmth to every occasion. 'Drains', however...well, I don't need to spell it out, do I?

Here are some 'draining' habits to avoid:

- Talking about yourself ad nauseam with no interest in anyone else's achievements, problems or topics;
- Only focusing on life's woes and cares;
- Leaving the television on (at full blast) when someone comes to visit;
- Taking an extended phone call when you have a visitor;

- Failing to edit out superfluous detail in a story you are recounting- we do not need endless point-by-point minutiae!!
- Greeting younger people who are busy with work, marriage, children, domestic chores but have taken the time and trouble to visit you with: *"I thought you had forgotten the way", or "You never have time for me these days since you met her/him", or "I thought you had forgotten all about me", etc;*
- Prioritising programmes on television or having other 'more important people' to visit, instead of allowing people who care about you and wish to see you call round. Then having the audacity to say, *"Oh, I never see you any more";*
- When someone asks you how you are, you actually tell them- in great detail, at great length, until they are bored rigid, but you show no interest in the other person's well-being;
- Dropping hints that they may be mentioned in your will, but, of course, *"that depends"* (i.e. emotional blackmail);
- Taking <u>any</u> point raised during a conversation as an opportunity to talk about your own past achievements, life history or stories;
- Grimacing, shrugging your shoulders or even criticising the gift someone has so kindly given you.

I could go on, but I think you get the gist!

Marie de Hennezel points out that people who have a network of relationships live longer than others, but, as she goes on to say, these relationships endure because they are very agreeable to be around. So let's all cultivate the art of being an agreeable 'radiator'.

What are some of the other traits I found in my radiant participants?

Giving to Others

In my study, I discovered that most of the participants spent some time each week in activities where giving was more important than receiving. These included voluntary sector work, Church activity and/or caring for ill or disabled partners and/or friends.

As Susan said, *"Loving Don (her husband who suffers from Parkinson's) fully and completely is what gives me my zest for life."* She continues, *"My volunteer work is as a caregiver for Don, and it's a labour of love."*

This is echoed by Ann who writes, *"I am a Lion (voluntary organisation) and we are always doing things for other people. I feel I am giving back to society for I have been lucky."*

This supports the findings of the Longevity Project which studied the lives of 1,528 people from 1921 over the following 90 years. The researchers discovered that those who were committed in their relationships, who tried to help others and were giving (rather than taking) in their attitudes towards others, lived longer than those who merely felt cared for. (Friedman and Martin, 2011)

For several committed Christians in my study, an important part of their lives involves giving of themselves to others via teaching, charity work, coaching, training leaders, welcoming new members and helping in the Church coffee shop, etc. The benefits they cited include: purpose and stimulation (Norma); providing zest for life (Sue S.); reaching out to others (Kate); finding an extended family (Elizabeth), and sharing with others (Betty S.).

So, just doing something regularly for others out of goodwill is actually good for us as well as benefiting others. In the words of the Aymara tradition:

'The only thing that survives after death is all that we have given.'

This might be a point to consider in your forward planning.

Enjoy the company of younger people

My participants all seemed to relish the company of younger people, including grandchildren and friends.

Their youth seemed to boost their spirits, and, far from finding young people irritating or annoying, they commented on the pleasure they gained from being with them.

In Janet's words, *"Seeing the enthusiasm and success of my grandchildren in their chosen paths"* is what boosts her spirits.

Joanna on her 80th birthday, August, 2011

Conversely, participant, Joanna (aged 80), with her customary twinkle in her eye, said to me the other day, *"Oh, I've stopped going to my exercise class."* When I asked her why, she laughed, *"It's full of old people moaning on about their problems- really boring!"*

For some time now, neuroscientists and psychologists have been aware of the important role that empathy plays in our interactions with others. Put succinctly, when we are around people who are upbeat and positive, those of us who are sensitive and empathic seem to internalise or even match some of that emotion so we are affected in a positive way by the encounter. On the other hand, when we are around toxic, difficult or boring people we often walk away feeling down in the dumps ourselves because we begin to reflect the emotion we have picked up from them (i.e. they drain us). Highly sensitive people may also be prone to over-identification, which is sometimes described by psychologists as 'emotional contagion.'

So, seeking the company of young people and/or uplifting people is beneficial to our well-being because we capture some of their buoyancy and energy. Is that something to add to your plan?

This leads us to my next finding:

Choose your company wisely

Clearly, the participants had already identified some of the above points, albeit at an informal level. Again and again, I was told that they are very choosy about who they socialise with. Scientists have coined a phrase to describe this: **'emotional**

selectivity'. For example, in Lewis Wolpert's study (2011), he found that being more selective about whom we spend time with is a key factor in raising our levels of happiness and maximising our cheeriness. So, don't feel guilty about reducing the amount of time you spend with people who make you feel miserable or anxious. You have the right to be choosy.

People the participants deliberately avoid include: *boring people, loud people, miserable, negative, controlling bullies, grouchy people and those who delight in conflict or malicious gossip.*

The reasons they give include: *'they fatigue me'; 'they cause trouble'; 'I like to avoid arguments'.*

I find it interesting that these ladies, who are all so lovely to be with, are very clear about avoiding those who can eat away at their self-esteem and emotional well-being.

However, sometimes we may find it difficult to totally avoid 'difficult people', so some of the strategies offered below may help you to deal with such situations. Just bear in mind that you do have the right to protect yourself and your health from their toxicity.

Minimising exposure. For example, visit a person who is grouchy and miserable, but limit the time you are there to 20 minutes and you will feel more in control of the situation.

Do something practical for him/her. Follow Maureen's advice and *'help those who are less fortunate'*. Perhaps wash up or fetch something they need, etc. The bonus here is that you are not a 'captive audience' listening to their woes if you are up and doing something active. Learn to cultivate the art of 'detached listening'.

Use your buffer shield. Imagine you are surrounded by bouncy, tough plastic. Any harsh words, criticisms or moans just bounce away and they don't get inside you.

Do not get 'hooked in' by their games. Try to retain an emotional distance in their company. Look on with compassionate interest as an observer (or imagine you are their psychotherapist) and make active listening noises such as "Oh, really", "Oh, I had no idea", "Mmm" (with nodding to show you are listening).

Learn to respond differently. As we discussed in Chapter 1, there are many things in our lives which we can't control, especially people. But, we can learn to control how we respond to them. Learning to distance yourself emotionally will help you to stay calm and keep the 'flight or fight' response under control, and, maybe, if we try hard enough, we can even acquire compassion towards them.

Just make sure you spend time with the 'radiators' afterwards!!

What are your current strategies? Could they be improved?

Jot down your thoughts here:

The importance of touch

Several participants mentioned massage as one of their 'treats'. The benefits they identified from it included: feeling relaxed and refreshed; relief of aches and pains; comforted; relaxed and happy, and '*they keep me limber*'.

I think these are very important points and perhaps relate to one of our basic human needs: the importance of touch. I found myself wondering what happens when we are older, perhaps living alone- do we still want and need to have our naked skin touched and caressed? Is sensuality something we still long for?

Marie de Hennezel (2011) tackled the question of sex in old age in her book and discovered that this was almost a taboo subject.

However, if the plethora of advertisements in 'Saga' magazine and 'Mature Times' placed by the over 50's is anything to go by, our need for romance and someone to cuddle remains important in our golden years. As Marie de Hennezel has discovered, our hearts do not age, and there is plenty of evidence that we can go on enjoying touch and sensuality right to the end of our lives.

Rather amusingly, Marie de Hennezel points out that it is often people's offspring who have a problem with the very idea of their elderly parents wanting to have any kind of sex life. A very elegant lady in her 70's told me a while ago that she met a nice man on a cruise, and she had arranged to meet up with him for a holiday. When she told her daughter that she must rush off to buy some pretty new underwear, her daughter was absolutely horrified. *"OMG, Mum! That's gross!"* was her outraged response.

There are many ways of experiencing the joy and pleasure of being touched and reciprocating in turn. But, just like our brain power, which we will discuss in Chapters 7 and 8, it is a case of *'Use it or lose it'*. Plenty of research supports the idea that touch and physical pleasure with another person promote well-being, the release of oxytocin (often referred to as 'the love hormone') and enhanced self-esteem. When researching this topic, Lewis Wolpert (2011) discovered that people who are healthy in old age are twice as likely to have a high libido, and they are also more likely to enjoy regular sex. However, as Friedman and Martin (2011) point out, there is a 'chicken and egg' conundrum here. People in stable, sexually satisfying relationships have certainly been found to live healthier and longer lives, but scientists still do not know what is causing what.

So, in the meantime, try to discover what you want and need, whatever your age. Open your mind to using all your senses, be adaptable, **focus on what you <u>can do</u>, and enjoy it!!!**

The power of laughter

I can truly say that I laughed and laughed during all our interviews. What a marvellous sense of humour these ladies have! And, what a tonic a shared laugh can be.

Of course, we can laugh when we are alone, but, when we are out and about in the company of positive people we smile more, laugh more, and have a heightened sense of well-being. Martin Seligman (2011) points out in his discussion of 'flourishing', that most of the fun and laughter we enjoy happen when we are with other people, not alone. That is one of the reasons why socialising with positive, fun people is so good for us.

As we will discuss in more depth in Chapter 9, Seligman contends that a key component of well-being is that sense of 'connectedness' with others.

So, like all these participants, **make time** to join activities, clubs, courses, luncheon clubs, Church, comedy nights, coach outings ...whatever takes your fancy, and enjoy a **good laugh**. Kate's family and friends have given her the nickname, *'Mrs. Never-in'*, but, as she and the other participants told me, getting out and about regularly is crucial to their emotional well-being. Kate said: *"Tell them, in your book, that becoming reclusive is the worst thing you can do because you go into yourself and dwell on your troubles."*

On the other hand, sometimes we all need a **shoulder to cry on.**

Having a strong network of close friends and/or family with whom we meet simply because we love them and their company was mentioned by **all** the participants.

As Ann has discovered, *"Talking with my friends over lunch is all the support I need if I ever feel down."*

Within these relationships, carefully nurtured and tended over the years, we provide and receive a reciprocal opportunity to share our 'trials and tribulations' as well as our exciting or humorous events. But the key word here is **'reciprocal'**. What can be worse than someone who phones and only talks about his/her problems but shows no interest in yours?

The ladies in this study are 'tuned in' and socially adept. They are true confidantes, and, according to Howard Friedman and Leslie Martin's research (2011), we all need those in our lives. These close relationships take time and effort to build over the years, but for those who do invest and give in this way, the rewards are a heightened sense of well-being, and, for many, a longer life.

Looking to the Future

It will be interesting to see what solutions the 'baby-boomers' come up with when they reach old age and need support. Here are some of the suggestions offered by younger people and students:

1. Buy a retirement villa somewhere warm, divided up into flatlets to be shared with a group of friends with resident nurses/ carers when the time comes, a communal recreational area, space for visitors and a garden [Annie Davies];
2. Take in a young student who, in exchange for free lodgings, will do some jobs around the house, keep you company sometimes, and escort you to the theatre, etc. [Zoe];
3. Shared, supported homes for vegetarians and vegans (rather than endless meals of stew and mince) [Sally];
4. A University of the Third Age Campus with good quality accommodation, interesting lectures from both guest lecturers and fellow residents, communal areas, clubs, activities, classes, sport, outings, halls with facilities such as bars, cinemas, swimming pools, golf courses, fishing areas, walking areas, spas, shops, libraries, ITC, hotel-like accommodation for visiting friends and relatives, restaurants, cafes, supermarkets, and video conferencing. These facilities would be very well appointed, comfortable, and somewhere NOT obviously institutionalised, but giving a range of social, educational, physical input and support [Annie Hughes];
5. Using the television set as a means of communication with the outside world via internet access. By using the remote control navigating will be straightforward. Social networking will be a feature with localised groups. With video facility, such as Skype, people will be able to speak with each other and see each other. This enables people to contact each other if they are not feeling well or need some shopping done. It is possible to check that someone is not lying down on the floor. This means there is also a source of contact for friendship and help [Neil]
6. Double beds in care homes, just in case... [Tim].

What creative ideas do you have? Ask your friends and family what they can envisage. Clearly, if we are to live our lives to the full, we will have to use our imaginations to get what we want and then put our ideas forward to politicians. Otherwise, we may end up with the kinds of provision which are currently failing far too many people.

In Conclusion

In this chapter, we have seen the importance of socialising, cultivating and nurturing good relationships and being the kind of person other people will want to be around for the duration. It is clear that finding people with whom we can feel a close connection and positive relationships must be a priority for us all.

We are all different, and what suits one person might be totally at variance with what suits another, but, good relationships really do matter.

Time to Reflect:

First, consider which aspects of your social life you are happy with. Which aspects seem to provide you with the kinds of joy and comfort expressed in this chapter?

Now, think about two things you can and will do to improve on this.

Next, consider your relationships.

Who are the people with whom you feel a strong sense of 'inter-connectedness'? Whose company do you most enjoy? Who are the 'radiators' in your life?

How can you arrange to spend more time with them? (This may include using 'Skype' for those who live far away or if it is difficult for you to get out and about.)

Who have you touched or hugged this week? Who has hugged you? Do you need increased opportunities to experience touch and/or sensuality in your life? If so, how will you achieve this?

Next, who would you call if you were having a crisis?

Who would call you in similar circumstances?

Is it time to make some kind of 'pact' with a few people (especially if you live alone) to have this kind of reciprocal arrangement?

What do you currently do to help others? Could you increase this?

Realise that you can't make people change, and self-protection is the key! So, how will you deal with potentially 'toxic' people?

Finally, is there any work you need to do in order to make yourself a more agreeable 'radiator' to be around? If so, start today- it's never too late! But only you can do it!

And- remember (as the popular slogan says), *"Be nice to your children; they will choose your nursing home one day."*

I would add: be especially nice to your daughters (and sons) – in-law!!!

How about trying social singing? It is no wonder that community choirs and 'rock choirs' are becoming so popular. There is nothing more exhilarating than singing with other people and learning to create beautiful music together. So, pluck up the courage and go along to a group in your locality. Join the thousands of people who have discovered the joy of singing in a group. Fun, laughter and a sense of connectedness with kindred spirits await you!

7 Make the Most of the Brain You Now Have

Despite their wide range of interests and the very alert, focused, lively conversations I had with them, some of the research participants expressed concerns about their memory. In particular, they noticed that their short term memory and their ability to recall names and words were not as good as they used to be. Some commented on an annoying tendency to find themselves in a room and forgetting what they have come for. If you are 50+, you may have already experienced some similar 'mature moments' and wondered what causes them.

So, what can current research teach us abut how to keep our brain in good shape? And, is it all 'doom and gloom' after 70?

Plasticity – our lifelong ability to create and change neural circuits

We have 100 billion of brain cells (or neurons), and they are often referred to as our 'grey matter'. Exciting research from neuroscience reveals the enormous potential number of connections which can be made between them. It has been discovered that we do not lose large numbers of neurons as was hitherto believed. Indeed, as Barbara Strauch (2010) points out, we can continue to create new neurons (a process called ***neurogenesis***) until we die. So, in theory, we can assume that we can continue to learn throughout our lives.

The brain is capable of continually reorganising itself by pruning back what we **don't need** (i.e. 'de-cluttering' to keep the brain more alert and efficient) and making new connections (our **'white matter'**) as we adapt to changing circumstances throughout our lives, not just when we are young. We also know that the amount of myelin (which surrounds the connecting axons to help to conduct messages between neurons) increases in the frontal and temporal lobes until our 50's and 60's. Until recently, it was thought that production of myelin stopped at adolescence. Now, researchers have discovered this is not the case. It is this increase in connectivity which is thought to contribute to 'wisdom' in later life.

Therefore, the plasticity of the brain can be considered a **dynamic**, mutable, versatile process. Norman Doidge (2007) suggests that it is useful to think of the brain, not as an empty vessel to fill up, but rather as a hungry animal which needs feeding.

Indeed, it is more accurate to refer to people in their 70's and over as: **sagacious, learned, wise, knowing, erudite, well-informed, well-read, elders of the community**, rather than as '*pensioners with decaying brains*'. Of course, the brain changes over the years: younger people's reaction and processing times are quicker, but, as Barbara Strauch tells us, research shows that older people have:

- a better, wider vocabulary;
- improved problem solving capacity because we use both sides of brain;
- better analytical skills;
- more rational, less impulsive decision making;
- good long-term memory;
- increased ability to make accurate judgments about people and finances;
- **WISDOM** (knowledge for dealing with life's problems, including conflict resolution).

This is a much more positive view of growing older, isn't it? Something to note is that much previous research took place in care homes; therefore, it was not totally representative of the wider community.

So, yes, our brains change over the years, but, as Ellen Langer (2010) says, change is not the same as decay!!! Our cognitive functioning may be different in middle-age onwards, but we are certainly not decrepit as a consequence.

A good question to ask yourself is: **which would I rather have – my 20 year- old brain, or the mature, sagacious, wise, experienced one that I am now proud to own?** When I ask older audiences this question, very few people have voted for the 20 year-old brain. Yes, we would all love to have our fast processing times back again, but look at what we have gained in middle age onwards.

Find new, challenging projects and interests

However, to fully reap the benefits of the brain's plasticity, there is **effort** involved. (This is the quid pro quo!!)

Norman Doidge and others suggest that we must seek out new opportunities to learn **new** skills and acquire **new** knowledge. Merely continuing to replay familiar skills is not quite enough. By the time you reach middle age, much of what you do is carried out on **autopilot** which can make the brain lazy. Compare this era with earlier periods in your life such as starting your new career, becoming a parent for the first time, studying to improve your qualifications, etc. These were all 'steep learning curves', and your brain was firing on all cylinders to keep up. But, as Norman Doidge says, by the time we are 70, it may be many years since we fully exercised our brains. What we have to find are **new** projects which will give the brain a reason to work harder again.

The key is to stimulate the brain frequently for optimum efficiency, and make sure that **effort, concentration and intense focus** are involved. A useful way to think of this is moving up from 2nd to 5th gear. This makes our brains fire up, especially the all-important frontal lobes. It also stimulates the production of brain chemicals (e.g. acetylcholine and dopamine) which facilitate neurotransmission of signals between brain cells. In addition, learning new things increases blood flow to the brain and builds up **cognitive reserve** which can, potentially, offer protection from later degeneration. In a nutshell, novelty and cognitive challenge ward off atrophy.

However, although we can benefit by choosing **novel** things which will challenge us, they must also be activities we will **really enjoy** in order to sustain our motivation.

So, take a look at the suggestions below. They are all sufficiently challenging to stimulate the kind of brain activity recommended by the researchers.

Which of these are you already doing?

- Learning a new language: Michael Merzenich, a leading researcher in the field of neuroplasticity, believes that this is an excellent neural activity to tune up the brain. (Cited in Doidge, 2007) As a keen linguist, Jessie knows all about the cognitive benefits of foreign language studies.

- Learning to play a musical instrument (for the same reason given above)
- A new physical activity involving fairly complex sequences such as T'ai Chi, Pilates, Yoga, or a new dance which involves highly focused attention (and controlled breathing)
- Studying a new subject at a sufficiently challenging level (e.g. University of the Third Age, WEA, Lifelong Learning, Open University, etc.)

Jessie Robertson

- Reading a **new** author, newspaper, etc.
- Doing the crossword in a more challenging newspaper
- Learning a new complex board, card, computer or word game
- Attending stimulating new cultural events
- Making a career change (which could include voluntary work when you retire)

Which other activities do you currently engage in to stimulate your brain?

As we have discovered, the participants in my research all seem to be 'novelty seekers', and most of them regularly engage in new (sufficiently challenging) activities which stimulate the brain. Indeed, many of them started new projects **after** they retired, and they have continued to do so ever since. In Chapter 10, we will return to this important theme.

You may be wondering why 'brain training' computer programmes have not been mentioned. The reason for that is because, as yet, research does not indicate that there is sufficient <u>transfer</u> to everyday cognitive activity. However, new research by Michael Merzenich is yielding very encouraging results in his 'Posit Science' programme. (Cited in Doidge, 2007) Undoubtedly, future developments will enable such programmes to be of lasting, transferable benefit to our brains. In the meantime, if you find you derive some benefit from 'brain training', do continue, but also add some of the suggestions above to extend your daily routine.

In addition, include some form of sufficiently active exercise to increase blood flow to the brain and encourage the birth of new neurons. As we discussed in Chapter 4 (Keep Moving), the eminent neuroscientist, Fred Gage, recommends trying to engage in some kind of exercise for 30 minutes a day which will stimulate the dentate gyrus and encourage new neural growth. (The dentate gyrus is a small section of the hippocampus which is crucial for memory function.) So, walk whenever you can, and include whatever form of exercise you enjoy in your daily programme. If we want to prevent brain atrophy, Norman Doidge (2007) points out that one of the most important things is to avoid being immobile for lengthy periods of time.

How will you extend what you are currently doing?

Aim for a **variety** of stimulating, new activities to enrich your life and provide new challenges for **<u>different</u>** parts of the brain. Ellen Langer (2010) exhorts us to open our minds to what we **CAN DO now**, rather than dwelling on what we <u>used</u> to do! **It's time, perhaps, to rediscover a passion for learning.**

So, identify TWO new things you will definitely do, and make a note of the DATE when you will begin on your calendar (which should be today or tomorrow, otherwise it will slip from your agenda):

1.

2.

And, if a 'friend' asks you why on earth you are learning to Salsa dance *'at your age'* and they tell you must be out of your mind, respond sweetly (but assertively) that you have no intention of losing your mind and that's exactly WHY you are doing it. Robert Fulghum (2007) said in one of his essays: '*I seek the sharp, scary pleasure that comes from beginning something new- that challenges my mind, my body and my spirit all at once.*'

That is why he took up tango at the age of 70!!! So, what's your excuse for not trying something new? Don't allow fear or embarrassment to hold you back.

So far, we have seen that the mature brain **is** capable of learning and memorising. What we will examine in the next chapter is **how** we might make fullest use of that capacity. Which practical strategies will be most useful when we are learning and trying to remember important things in our everyday lives?

8 Use It or Lose It: Practise Your Memory Strategies

George Burns (the American comedian) once said: ***"By the time you're eighty years old you've learned everything. You only have to remember it!"***

That is the challenge we will explore in this chapter. I have organised some of the many findings from research into 7 key words, the first letter of each, when combined, spells 'PROTEST'. I hope you will find this acronym a useful memory aid.

First, identify your current strengths and 'targets':

Many people in the 70+ age-group tell me that they are worried about their 'memory'. But, what we have to realise is that there are **different types** of memory, such as:

- Episodic memory- of events in our past, both recent and distant
- Semantic memory- for factual knowledge, words and names
- Procedural memory- for how to do things, such as driving a car

In addition, some of us have strong visual memory for pictures and faces, whilst others find it easier to recall auditory input such as voices or melodies. Some people can remember long sequences of numbers, and others have more extensive recall of words.

Most of us discover that we have strengths and other aspects where we are not quite so 'hot' at remembering. All too often, I find that people tend to focus too much on what they forget, and underestimate what they can remember.

So, it is useful to reflect on the things you find it **easy** to remember, and then identify a few 'targets'- aspects you are going to put some effort into improving.

Here are some ideas to get you started:

- Faces
- Names
- Visual pictures
- Dates
- Numbers
- Sequences
- Melodies
- Episodes from long ago
- Poems and/or songs
- Facts from hobbies and interests
- Skills- how to do things such as drive your car, cook, knit, play the piano, etc
- Recent events
- Vocabulary
- Other

How did you get on? Were you pleasantly surprised to discover that there are more things which you regularly remember than you realised?

It is also worthwhile mentioning that memorisation involves **4 stages:**

1. Taking in and processing the information.
2. Retaining it in the short-term memory.
3. Encoding it in your 'working memory' and thence to your long-term memory.
4. Recalling or retrieving it.

In order for memorisation to be as effective as possible, we need to ensure that our strategies at each stage work well. The rest of this chapter will help you to improve on your 'target' areas.

P Plasticity –

It will be useful to read Chapter 7 and the important findings about neuro-plasticity before you tackle the next section. The key discovery researchers have made is that we can continue to improve our brain capacity throughout our lives thanks to its plasticity, but only if we make the **effort** which this involves.

But, what kind of effort will be most effective?

R Relax–

Dominic O'Brien (eight times World Memory Champion) describes anxiety as the 'enemy of remembering'. Cortisol (produced during times of stress) can impair our concentration, so it is very important to deal with stress. Before he memorises anything or engages in memory contests, he makes sure that he is thoroughly relaxed.

The optimum state for learning is when we are **relaxed but focused.** A key consideration is our breathing, to ensure a good supply of oxygen to the brain. Dominic practises daily meditation to relax, focus and slow down the brain waves, filter out constant inner dialogues (including self-criticism and self-doubts) and focus completely on the here and now.

Activity:

List the ways in which you currently experience total relaxation:

Now, plan some other activities which will help you to completely relax.

My daily **relaxation will now include:**

And- don't forget the importance of LAUGHTER every day!!!!

O Organise it –

Many of us already use **mnemonics** (or memory aids) to help us remember things.

The rhyme we learnt at school: '30 days hath September ...', and the 'Alphabet song' are examples of mnemonics. The acronym, 'PROTEST', which we are using here acts as 'pegs' for the information I am presenting to you which organises key points and aids recall.

Various experiments reveal that organising items into **categories** is also helpful. For example, we can group similar items in a shopping list together to aid recall:

Fruit: apples, oranges, lemons.
Vegetables: carrots, leeks, potatoes.
Toiletries: soap, shampoo, etc.

Tony Buzan advocates the use of **mind-maps**, and I certainly find them useful when I am giving talks. The example below shows the mind-map I used to help me to organise one of the talks I give on memory. I never need to use notes when I deliver presentations since I discovered mind-maps.

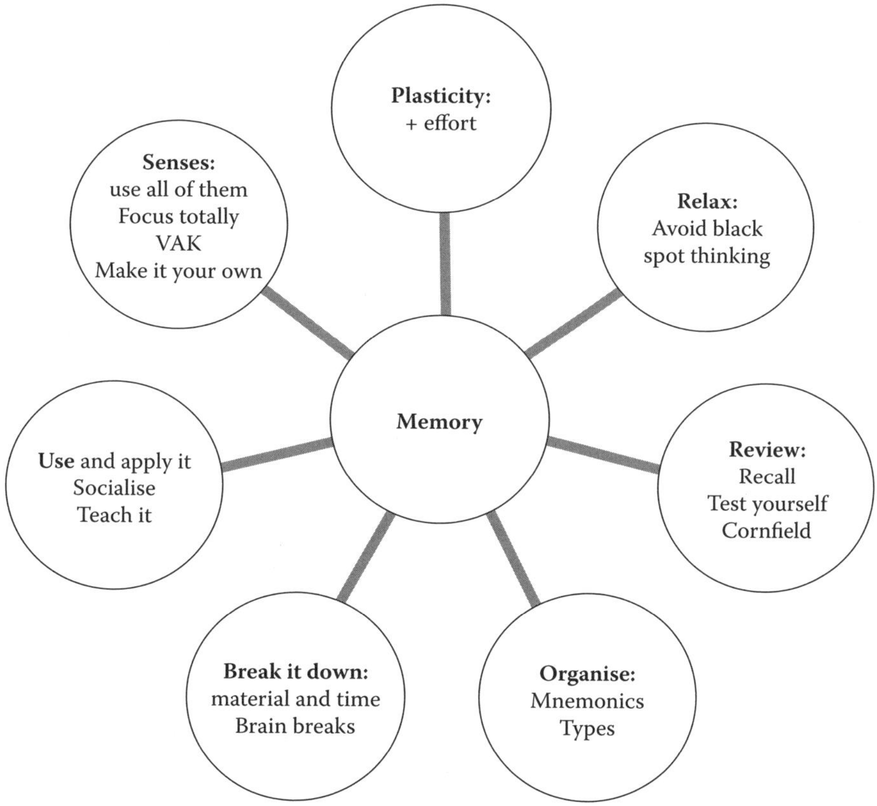

Those of you who prefer **linear sequences** can organise your material as 'bullet points', rather than 'spidergram' mind-maps. You can also construct different shapes of mind-maps to suit the material you are working with. (See Tony Buzan's publications for ideas, or use some of the 'organisation' or 'diagram charts' in your computer.)

All of these strategies enable us to organise the information in a way that strengthens the connections and links between old and new material. The effort we put into **processing** and engaging with the material to construct our organising frameworks will also aid recall. But we are all different, so have fun experimenting, and discover what works for you- there is no **one way** in which to organise material.

T Test yourself – use ACTIVE RECALL ('rehearsal')

Research by Ebbinghaus many years ago revealed that, without review and active recall within 24 hours, we forget **50-80%** of what we learn. If you want to retain new information, keep reviewing it. **With each revision, the impression on our memory deepens**. Professor Robert Winston (Doctor, scientist and TV presenter) uses the useful analogy of a corn field to explain this: each time you walk the same pathway through a cornfield the impression you make becomes more permanent.

However, in order to be successful, our revision of material must be **active!!** Merely reading through it again is less likely to be effective, especially as we age.

So- **test yourself**. For example, after reading the newspaper, watching a film or documentary on TV or the news, or attending at talk, try to recall a few key points. Then test yourself later that same day, one day after, 2/3 days later, one week later, and so on. This simple strategy strengthens the connections or synapses between the brain cells, and reactivates the frontal lobes which can become 'sluggish'. The secret is to do a little, often. Look on it as a fun exercise- do not get stressed by it!!

Also, if you know in advance that you will test yourself, you will **engage** more with the task in hand, **pay more attention**, and thus memorise it. Therefore, read or watch television with questions in mind, talk about interesting programmes with your friends, pretend that you are a book, film or TV 'critic', and write reviews, etc.

All these activities will enhance your short-term memory **and** your confidence.

E Engage totally –

One of the frequent problems cited by both the researchers and the ladies in this study is that, as we get older, we get more easily distracted which interferes with our concentration. People tell me of 'internal chatter' or 'noisy, busy brains'. Does that ring a bell with you?

What can we do to counter this tendency?

Focus fully on the task in hand when you do things you want to remember. Forget multi-tasking if you want to concentrate! Ellen Langer (2010) advocates the use of mindfulness- being fully present in the moment, as we have discussed in previous chapters.

Dominic O'Brien and other 'masters of memory' use **meditation** to aid their concentration and become totally centred. As Norman Doidge (2007) points out, our memory of something will only be as clear as the original signal. Thus, if we are not concentrating very well, it is no wonder that we forget things. We need to focus well to register new events with accuracy, strength and sharpness. Otherwise, our recall will be muddled and cloudy.

This is another good reason to learn new material or skills: when we are totally absorbed in something which fascinates us, and we are operating at 5th gear, our brains are less likely to veer off into internal 'chatter'.

It is common sense, but worth mentioning, that a healthy diet, exercise and sufficient fluid intake are all important too. (See Chapters 4 and 5.)

Also, take frequent 'brain breaks', especially when you are watching TV, otherwise we can develop the bad habit of 'drifting' into our internal world which can become our 'default setting'. We are all different, but the average optimum concentration span for most adults is around 20-30 minutes. So, get up, move around, drink some water, and return to the task in hand totally alert and engaged.

One of the best ways is engage your brain is to:

S **Socialise –**

Barbara Strauch (2010) comments that we have underestimated the importance of so-called 'simple' conversations. Yet, when we pause to analyse what goes on during conversation we realise that the brain is very activated. Amongst other things, it is using '5th gear' to: **organise, structure, sequence, clarify, concentrate, select appropriate vocabulary, edit, talk in an appropriate style to your audience, use active recall, etc., etc.**

Thus, we can see the importance of maintaining a good social life and networking with intelligent, **positive** people who want to do more than merely discuss aches and pains and the weather!!!!

But, be selective- choose your company wisely!!! Many of my participants discussed the value they derive from being with interesting, stimulating people from whom (and with whom) they can learn new things and discover novel points of view.

Use your social circles to share your knowledge: by doing so, you hugely increase the possibility that you will remember it. So... phone a friend to talk about the news or what you watched on TV or a book you are reading, visit a restaurant to use the new language you are learning, join a book group, go and dance the new steps, then teach them to someone else. Indeed, "*Teaching another person is one of the best ways to learn it*" is an old cliché, but true. So, do consider leading a U3A group if you have specialist skills and knowledge to share. (See 'Useful Contacts'.) Prioritise cultivating a good social life with interesting people and avoid the 'drains' we discussed in Chapter 6.

T Tip of the Tongue Moments ('TOTS') and what to do about them

How often do you find that the more you try to recall something (e.g. a name or a word we know but can't quite remember on the spot) the more it eludes you? Then, a few hours or even minutes later, when you relax, it comes to you easily? Or, how about those times we find ourselves in a room and we can't think why we have gone there?

Most of are familiar with these 'tip of the tongue' moments, including the middle-aged academic writers and researchers referred to in this book!!! Various causes may be cited which include:

- lack of focus, going into 'autopilot' mode or being distracted;
- having too much information and/ or many names to 'trawl through';

- names are stored in a different part of the brain from the information we have about the person, such as how they look, their profession, etc., so activating the connection between the two can take longer as we grow more 'senior';
- stress or anxiety- the more we worry about it, the worse it becomes.

The key thing to bear in mind is that this happens to be part of the changing nature of the brain. Yes, it is annoying, sometimes even embarrassing, but there is no need to worry. It is perfectly normal to experience some decline in what Allen Bragdon and David Gamon (2010) tactfully call '*mental nimbleness*.' In essence, we may just need more time to recall from our extensive vocabulary and list of names.

So, avoid **'black spot thinking'.** All too often, I find people become unduly worried about the relatively minor moments when they forget something, and fail to value the much more frequent occasions when they do remember all kinds of complex, difficult material. If you refer back to Chapter 1, you will recall our focus on managing our thinking by using Cognitive Behavioural Therapy. So, focus on what you **can** remember...otherwise we can get caught up in a vicious circle of negative thinking.

Some practical strategies to try:

Here are a few practical strategies to help with 'TOTS':

First of all **names**: The key is to create strong (even surreal, bizarre and funny) mental images to which you can link the name to your visual recall of the person.

For example, let's say you are introduced to a man called Ray Taylor. Perhaps he is a smiling ***'ray'*** of sunshine, and he is quite dapper in his dress, so you can think of his good ***'tailor'*** who kits him out. By using this strategy, we create a strong link between the abstract name, and the much easier to remember visual picture.

Now, devise a similar strategy to help you remember **my name!** (My photo will help you, and remember I am Scottish!)

Try out the same procedure for several other names, and you will find it increasingly easy to think of visual links. Indeed, make full use of the creativity and lateral thinking which are part and parcel of the older brain.

Next, let's try a similar procedure for a **word in a foreign language**. For example, if you sign up to a French class for the first time, you will find many words are similar to English so they are easy to recall (e.g. café, toilette, restaurant, chocolat). But, there will be words which bear little or no resemblance to English such as 'parapluie' (umbrella) which demand more effort to recall. If we break the word into two parts, 'para' is a bit like 'para' as in parasol, so we can visualise a lady with a lovely bright parasol, and 'pluie' sounds a bit like a bird calling 'plooee, plooee', so we can visualize a bird 'dropping' rain down on the lady as it flies around.

I know this sounds rather bizarre, but researchers such as Michael Raugh and Richard Atkinson (1975) have found that the more surreal, colourful and unusual the image, the more likely we are to remember the word. The reason they offer is that, when the word is coupled with interesting, memorable visuals, this provides a stronger neural footprint than the word alone.

Now try to devise your own visual mnemonic for 'la poubelle' (dustbin).

The key 'rules' for learning new words or names are:

Connect the familiar with unfamiliar, and use all your senses.

Observe closely – look at the detail. (Observational drawing is also an extremely useful focus exercise.)

Aurally – say it aloud so you can hear the word (Our American cousins do this when they are introduced to someone new.)

Kinaesthetically – write it down- act it out – mime it- do it.

Smell and taste can also be activated. For example, if you are learning the vocabulary for fruit, food names and vegetables in a new language, have the real objects in front of you so that you can smell them, taste them and hold them as you repeat the new words. This will strengthen the neural connections in your brain.

And, what about words which just won't come when you are conversing in English?

The other day I attended the opening of an art exhibition, and the lady (in her late 60's) who gave the opening speech provided an excellent address which was short, focused and sincere.

Afterwards, I was keen to congratulate her on her speech, but she was preoccupied and embarrassed because she had momentarily forgotten the word, 'dream', while she addressed the audience. I am not sure that she even recognised what a clever speech it was. Isn't that sad?

So, let me reiterate, no one else probably even notices our 'TOTS', and, if they do, they are probably very empathic because it happens to us **all**. Please, do not allow 'black-spot thinking' to dent your confidence. It is just not worth it.

In the meantime, continue to read widely, do your crosswords and other word puzzles, write poetry, letters, stories and converse regularly. The wider our vocabulary, the more likely we are to think of substitute words which are similar to the elusive one we are searching for. And, continuing to socialise will keep our accessible vocabulary active well into our senior years.

In conclusion, in this chapter, we have explored some strategies to assist our mature brains to work most effectively. But, we are all different, so do try different strategies to see what works for you!! As my Latin teacher used to say, "*Make it your own.*"

Now, set the book aside and, using the 'PROTEST' acronym to help you recall the 7 key strategies used in this chapter, see how much you can remember. You could record what you remember on your own mind-map or bullet points. Then, use active recall by testing yourself later, tomorrow, a few days hence, etc, to make your memory of the chapter more permanent.

In addition, try to include some of the tips discussed every day. Make a note of the strategies you have found useful on some 'post-its', and stick them around the house to remind you to get into the habit of using them. After a few weeks, they will become part of your daily routine and, hopefully, you will find your confidence in your memory growing.

To conclude

The good news discovered by recent research reveals that:

a) we **can** go on learning and remembering all our lives thanks to the plasticity of the brain, but,

b) passivity or becoming set in our ways quite simply does not work. We must put **effort** into keeping the brain in good working order, and use some of the strategies I have shared with you. **'Use it or lose it!'**

Of course, if you <u>think</u> your memory is going to fail as you age, this can become a self-fulfilling prophecy. It is only when we learn to value the power of the plasticity of our mature brain, and harness that power by learning new things, that we can look positively towards the future.

And- every time you see, hear or read someone making incorrect, negative assumptions about the brain capacity of older people, PROTEST loudly and correct them!!!!

If this book has inspired you to sing, try this for fun- my own version of the song, *'Memory,'* (with apologies to Trevor Nunn and Andrew Lloyd Webber):

Midnight, all alone in my bedroom,
I forgot what I came for,
Oh, I've lost it again!
But, let me focus and use my props to help me along,
And my memory will work again.

Every gal must relax each day,
And practise all her strategies.
Organise your mind-maps,
And meet with all the nice chaps,
And soon, your neurons will be zinging!

Get out there,
And find some new skills,
Your brain will love you,
And you know that you can.
Just steer clear of those 'drains' who try to bring you down,
Let your memory live again.

Ooh- I've just remembered what I came for!!!

9 Organise Your Time Effectively, But Be Spontaneous Too

If I had £10 for every time someone has said to me, "I don't know where my time goes" I would be a wealthy woman indeed.

In this chapter, we are going to find out exactly where your time goes so that you can decide if this is the best way in which to organise yourself. Then you will plan how to make your time-management even more effective (whilst allowing opportunities for spontaneous happenings).

I was astonished by the wide variety of activities and hobbies my participants engage in on a regular basis. Here are just some of them:

- **'Brain' activities:** reading, crosswords, word puzzles, University courses, learning foreign languages, writing columns for a local newspaper, local history outings, debates;
- **Physical activities:** gardening (including digging), walking (in some cases up to 8 miles!), rambling, hiking, gym, yoga, aerobics, swimming, ballroom dancing, cycling;
- **Work:** a few of the participants still work part-time, and love it;
- **Helping others:** voluntary work, Church activities (e.g. meeting and greeting, working in the Coffee Shop), helping less fortunate people, supporting family in their activities, caring for partners;
- **Creative and cultural activities:** sewing, playing musical instruments, choir, home cooking and baking, keeping scrap-books of family history and events, painting and art classes, listening to beautiful, inspiring music, concerts, study tours to art galleries and operas, theatre;
- **Enjoying the wonders of nature:** bird watching, wildlife excursions, walking and rambling, visiting lovely gardens;

- **Socialising:** outings, eating out with partners and/or friends, meeting or talking with friends on 'Skype', e-mail or on the phone, Church groups, luncheon clubs;
- **Spiritual activity:** Bible study, prayer, Church;
- **Other:** travel (many participants have travelled extensively since retirement), various beauty treatments and massage/ reflexology…phew!!!

I wonder if you are feeling exhausted just reading that list? But, far from tiring them out, all the participants reported that these activities **give** them *'a purpose', 'energy and vitality', 'satisfaction and stimulation'*. No 'couch potatoes' there!

On the contrary, these ladies are flourishing and are filled with a self-reported feeling of meaning in their lives. This seems to confirm Martin Seligman's latest theory (2011) that there are five aspects to well-being:

- **Positive emotion** (e.g. pleasure, joy and comfort)
- **Engagement** in an activity which induces a feeling of 'flow' or total absorption (e.g. when we paint, dance, write a poem, make love)
- **Meaning** – that feeling that what we do serves a bigger purpose than merely (in Seligman's words) *'fidgeting 'til death'* or amusing ourselves. For the participants, meaningful activity includes helping others, Church or voluntary work, caring for sick partners.
- **Accomplishment (or achievement)**, which is the feeling the participants report when they complete a painting, decorate a room, learn new skills such as languages, e-mailing or dancing, finish a crossword.
- **Positive relationships** which we discussed in Chapter 6.

Seligman uses the mnemonic, ***'PERMA'***, to summarise his theory:

*P*ositive emotion
*E*ngagement
*R*elationships
*M*eaning
*A*ccomplishments

Reflection: Do your current activities provide adequate opportunities to 'flourish'?

It would be a good idea to write down all the activities in which you regularly engage and people with whom you frequently socialise. Identify which of them currently fulfil Seligman's five criteria for 'flourishing'. At the end of this chapter you will jot down some ideas for future planning, which will be especially useful if you are heading towards retirement.

POSITIVE EMOTIONS	
ENGAGEMENT in absorbing activities which give you 'flow'	
RELATIONSHIPS which are positive and enriching	
MEANING and purpose in your life	
ACCOMPLISHMENT and achievement	

What was noteworthy in their responses to my questions on how they divide their time is how **organised** the participants are. However, as we discovered in Chapter 2, they also like to make time for spontaneity, thus providing plenty of opportunity for what Susan refers to as *'serendipity'*. In other words, most of them try not to become too bound by stultifying or rigid routines.

So, where exactly does your time go?

Activity: Auditing your time expenditure

Keep a record over the next 3 or 4 days and record the time, what you were doing then, and any thoughts you have during the period recorded. (The chart in Appendix 3 can be photocopied for this purpose.)

Then reflect on what you have discovered:

- Are you pleased with this balance?
- Are you surprised by what you found?
- Were these days typical of other days, or were there exceptional circumstances?
- Were you disappointed when you saw the pattern of your time expenditure?
- What does this evidence suggest about how you currently use your time?
- What are you going to do differently?

Make a note of your responses to these questions below, then do the next activity.

Activity: How you were feeling during your daily activities

Referring to your record, reflect on how you were feeling at the time.

During which activities (or in whose company) did you experience negative feelings such as:

- Boredom?
- Tension or stress?
- Anger?
- Other-

Make a note of them in the chart below:

Boredom	Tension	Stress	Anger	Other

Think creatively about how you can use this information. How can you ensure that you use your time wisely to maximise positive emotions and minimise negative ones? Which activities will you prioritise to bring that *'feeling of accomplishment'* which Shelagh and the other participants think is so important? Which activities (or people) can you drop or decrease from your life if they are creating negative emotions for you?

Some questions to ask:

- Are some jobs taking longer than they should?
- What are your 'time robbers'? How can you minimise their impact?

- Are all these jobs necessary? Could some be done weekly (or even monthly) instead of daily? The most active of the participants appear to limit the time they spend doing housework, preferring to be out and about attending interesting, uplifting, stimulating activities and meeting people.
- How can you increase the amount of time you spend in pleasurable activity?
- Would planning ahead help? Perhaps a weekly planner like the example in Appendix 4 will be useful.
- Are you spending enough time with people whose company you really enjoy? Is this something to address?
- Are you spending too much time alone, or with people you don't really like very much, including those who 'drain' you?
- What about TV? Were you surprised by how much precious time is eroded on mindless TV watching? If so, it's time to take control and limit your TV watching to programmes which are **really** stimulating. None of the participants are TV 'addicts': they are far too busy doing more worthwhile things.

When we retire, these questions are particularly relevant, but do bear in mind that the **bad habits we have developed during our working lives** are not going to magically disappear overnight. When I asked younger people what they look forward to in their 70's and over, without exception, they said having time to do interesting things. But I wager that, for many 'work or housework addicts', finding that elusive balance will be just as difficult in retirement as it is right now. Equally, there is no guarantee that those who 'fritter time away' will be any more organised when they retire. Dorothy strongly recommends planning in advance for retirement, otherwise *"You will wake up on the Monday after you retire thinking: 'What on earth will I do with myself now?' Then, you end up watching TV all day long."*

As the words of Octavio Paz, the Mexican poet and novelist, remind us:

'With freedom, we also fall into a boundless abyss- that of ourselves.'

Find a Sensible Balance

So, what we all need to do is to realise that finding a balance is not a matter of choice: it is a matter of necessity if we are to live life to the full in our golden years.

It's time to finally give yourself permission to enjoy 'me-time' and engage in pursuits every day which replenish you, stimulate you and provide a feeling of satisfaction.

In Stephen Covey's book (1989), entitled *'The 7 Habits of Highly Successful People',* he tells a wonderful story about a man who is walking through a wood when he encounters another man sawing vigorously. The first man walks on and returns a while later where he finds the same man still sawing away but with no tangible result. The first man asks politely what the problem is- why is so little progress being made despite such hard work? In reply, the man sawing responds that the saw is blunt. Ah, thinks the first man, the solution is obvious- break off now and sharpen the saw and your task will be so much more effective. To this sensible suggestion, however, the second man replies, "But how can I break off to sharpen the saw when there is still so much work to be done?"

If there are chores which you absolutely hate doing, can you delegate them? Trade them with a friend who does not mind doing yours but loathes a few of her own? Is it time to employ a cleaner? If you have to do them yourself, set yourself a time-frame. It doesn't matter if they are not finished – call a halt as soon as the time limit is up. (Set an egg-timer to make sure.)

Do not become a slave to housework or gardening!!! Will you really be lying on your death-bed saying, "Oh, how I wish I had spent more time doing the dusting or the weeding"? **I do not think so!!!**

You are in charge of your time- you decide!!

Throughout this book, we have discussed the kinds of activities which we all need if we are to stay fit and well, both mentally and physically, in our old age.

Activity: How will you sharpen your saw?

From the list below, identify a few activities which you know will provide you with joy, well-being and a feeling of renewed energy:

- Socialising with interesting, stimulating, uplifting people
- Exercise, including yoga, T'ai Chi and Pilates
- Beauty treatments and caring for yourself
- Spiritual activity which can include meditation or prayer, and being fully present in the world of nature, as well as religious pursuits
- Total relaxation which can include massage
- Taking time out to count your blessings
- Going on a retreat
- Creative pursuits including music, painting, writing poetry, stories, memoirs, journal
- Learning new things just for the fun of it
- Sensual activity and/or sex
- Being around younger people
- Doing things of your choosing for other people
- Doing something which you know will give you a really good laugh
- **SINGING!!!**
- What my friend, Annie Hughes, refers to as '*disgraceful times*'
- Other:

How do you feel about making time for yourself? Guilty? Excited? Liberated? Worried? Anxious? Try to explore and analyse why you feel this way. Where do these feelings come from? Past experiences? Current obligations? Being at the grindstone too long? Enjoyment at being the one in control?

Whatever you discover, if you are going to live a healthy old age, you will need to learn how to renew your energies.

A useful slogan is:

RECREATION leads to RE-CREATION

I often use the analogy of a jug of water when I work with students and clients who have problems making time for renewal:

Imagine you are a jug of water. What happens if you keep pouring the water out all the time but you don't refill it? Answer: It runs dry. Do you really want to enter your precious hard-earned retirement dried up and blunt like an old saw?

So, let go of these bad habits from the past, work out a better way to spend your time and make time for renewal. Aim for a variety of activities, and you (and all those around you) will feel the positive difference this will make to the quality of your life.

What is stopping you? Perhaps some of the 'ah, buts' below ring a bell.

Ah, but...!

My husband doesn't know how to cook, so we'll starve to death if I don't do it.

Solution: Enrol him on a cookery course as his next birthday present, buy some 'ready-made' meals, eat salads, eat out more often, etc, etc.

I am the only one who does the cleaning well enough.

Solution: Teach your kids and partner how to clean well enough- look on it as essential life skills for the future. Also, realise that there is no one way to do things. They may choose to do the job differently from you. Learn to be satisfied with that.

I can't afford to go for a massage or beauty treatment.

Solution: As we discussed elsewhere, book an appointment at your local college of beauty or further education where you can get really nice treatments (under supervision) by students in training. Alternatively, join your nearest 'barter club' or set one up yourself; you do something for someone, and they reciprocate. You could also join a massage course with a friend or your partner so you can practise on each other. That could be great fun!

What are your 'ah, but' blocks to managing your time in a healthier way?

Write them down along with some solutions which you WILL put into practice. If you are stuck for solutions, discuss this with a friend, colleague or counsellor. If you find it difficult to assert your needs clearly, calmly and directly, there are lots of books and courses available on Assertiveness. Don't suffer in silence. (I have added two useful books to the list of 'Sources'.)

Finding creative solutions to our 'time-robbers' and 'ah, buts' can be immensely liberating. After being on my courses on stress and time-management, people tell me they can't imagine why they didn't choose better ways to manage time years ago. But, it's never too late. The oldest person attending my courses was in her late 70's, and, every time I see her in town, she tells me: *"I have never looked back since that course."*

When you finally learn to balance your time, most of you will feel so much better as you gain a **sense of being**, rather than feeling swamped by paperwork or an endless list of things **to do** like the person in the illustration below. Remember that we are **'human beings',** not **'human doings'**.

I am drowning in a sea of paper,
Suffocating
In a silent scream.

Of course, if you are a bit of a 'control freak', that might not be the case. We can all think of people who find it impossible to delegate, share or let go of tasks that grind them down. Why? Because they have to be in charge. In addition, they tend to play the 'victim' role and moan to whoever is listening about all the jobs they *'have'* to do. I used to live next door to such a person and what a misery she was! How sad to see people wasting their precious years of retirement on stultifying, boring domestic routines because they cannot let go.

Perhaps these famous words from Helen Keller (who was deaf, mute and blind) will persuade you to make the most of every day:

Use your eyes as if tomorrow you would be stricken blind. And the same method can be applied to other senses. Hear the music of voices, the song of the birds, the mighty strains of an orchestra, as if you would be stricken deaf tomorrow. Touch each object you want to touch as if tomorrow your tactile sense would fail. Smell the perfume of flowers, taste with relish each morsel, as if tomorrow you could never smell and taste again. Make the most of every sense.

And, as the participants said again and again, make the most of every day and be **fully present** in the moment. ***'Beauty, like happiness, occurs frequently. Not a day goes by in which we don't, for an instant, live in paradise.'*** (Jorge Luis Borges, the Argentinian writer and literary critic) Make sure you are not so busy with mindless routines and 'to do' lists that you miss <u>your</u> daily moments in paradise.

Activity:

Now plan what you are definitely going to do FROM THIS DAY ONWARDS in order to learn how to flourish in your golden years. Martin Seligman's acronym, 'PERMA', will help you to remember your ideas, but planning them in your diary is also essential. Otherwise, your dreams may never become reality.

What will give you-

POSITIVE EMOTIONS	
ENGAGEMENT in absorbing activities which give you 'flow'	
RELATIONSHIPS which are positive and enriching	
MEANING and purpose in your life	
ACCOMPLISHMENT and achievement	

And, how will you ensure that you leave sufficient flexibility for singing, spontaneity and 'serendipity'? Remember that over-timetabling can rob you of your zest for life.

10 Find New Projects and Goals

> *'If you want to find fulfilment, my friend, don't co-exist with life- embrace it!'*
>
> Jim Beggs

Throughout my research, I have been struck by the participants' love of novelty and new experiences. They all seem to take delight in actively seeking new challenges, and this is reflected in their vitality and zest for life.

In this chapter, we will explore how the participants embrace this golden chapter of their lives and then go on to formulate an individual action plan to inspire and motivate you in your life. This will be particularly important if you are retired or about to retire, but can be applied at any age.

What makes the 'golden chapter' so wonderful?

Again and again, when I asked the participants when they had felt most satisfied with their lives, they said **now**.

Here are a few examples to inspire you:

Kate: *"You can have a wonderful time in your 70's. Life* **can** *begin at 70!"*
Betty S.: *"You suddenly think- this is me, this is my time. I enjoy every day!"*
Mary: *"You are free to do your own thing, so you can do what you want to do."*
Shelagh: *"Strangely enough, the best time of my life is now."*

Although there are many differences in their life styles, there were several themes which they seem to have in common:

Seek out new experiences and always keep looking forwards rather than backwards

Taking Kate as an example, in her 70's she travelled extensively to Australia, New Zealand and Canada. On her trip to Canada, she travelled the whole country by bus, and, in New Zealand, she was back-packing!!! She also started keep-fit classes when she retired. I found all the participants enjoy novelty: they embrace, rather than shy away from, new experiences.

Have adventures and thrills

Susan and her husband, Don (who suffers from Parkinsons' disease) bought a motor-home only recently, and they drive to Arizona to spend the winter months there. They also love cruising, and have visited some exciting and unusual places on their travels.

Susan Dressel-Myers and husband, Don, bird-watching

Betty C.'s 'semi-retirement' appears to be a series of adventures and thrills. All the participants seem to launch into these new ventures fearlessly, confident that they will have a good time and cope with challenges along the way.

Search for new interests which will challenge you

For Shelagh, each new decade has created an opportunity to try out a new venture. In her 70's, she opened a coffee shop with her daughter, certain that she would rise to the challenge of cooking and standing on her feet for lengthy periods of time. Mary took up painting with the cheque she received from colleagues when she retired at the age of 60 from teaching. Norma told me: *"I've been a "late bloomer" in several things. I was raised strictly with no dancing. I took dancing lessons at 77 and remarried at 77 to my partner at the lessons. I also took up golf at 74 and joined a women's golfing league. So many of us born in the United States during the great depression learned the work ethic so thoroughly that we didn't allow much time for play even after things got better."* Sue S. just seems to thrive on the challenge of new projects and Church missions. She firmly believes that using her spiritual gifts in serving others gives her a zest for life.

They all have a great sense of 'I'll have a go' and 'Why not?' which is incredibly inspiring.

Be open to meeting new people

Although the participants all have long-term friendships which they value most highly, they also like to meet new people who may have different points of view and interests. For example, Ann became a 'Lion' several years ago, and she has welcomed the opportunity to *"get a buzz from meeting new people."* Similarly, Betty S. loves her Church work as a member of a Welcoming Team, and finds enormous pleasure from making new people feel welcome. There is that sense of feeling open (not closed) to the new perspectives and *"fresh conversations"* (D.) that meeting new people can bring into their lives.

Find a project which has a purpose bigger than self-gratification

Feeling needed, helping others, and having a sense of mission or purpose permeates their lives. These are not egoists or self-interested attention seekers. A key feature is their desire to enrich other peoples' lives in some way, which can be through voluntary, Church or paid work, or by caring for family and partners. I find it interesting that this aspect is also emphasised by Howard Friedman and Leslie Martin (2011) in their study of Longevity. They talk about giving back through community activities, having a purpose in your life, and finding meaningful direction to give your life a sense of importance. It seems that giving to others, as Seligman (2003) discovered in his research, enables us to live a meaningful life, not just a life characterised by ephemeral, fleeting pleasures, *'fidgeting 'til death'*. A strong sense of purpose generates positive energy and direction which are often lacking in a life characterised by hedonistic self-gratification.

Love learning

They all delight in learning new things. Whether it be from travel, meeting new people, attending classes, reading extensively, theatre, music, etc., etc., they love to have their minds and imaginations stimulated. As Rusty commented: *"Keep yourself involved passionately in whatever interests you."* I find her use of the word, *'passionately'* worthy of particular attention. When I spoke with the role models about their hobbies, classes and what they were learning, they seemed to light up with almost childlike enthusiasm as they told me about it. You will recall this quote from Robert Fulghum (2007) when we discussed the brain in Chapter 7: *'I seek the sharp, scary pleasure that comes from starting something new- that calls on all my resources and challenges my mind, my body, and my spirit, all at once.'*

Not for them, resting on their laurels, and moseying along in 2nd gear: the participants seem to need, and actively seek out, new learning experiences. For about half the group, this includes acquiring some computer skills.

All the above may be summed up by Shelagh when she says: *"Every decade brings a new milestone and with it a new challenge. You have to celebrate them and accomplish something. I want to feel that my life has not been wasted."*

So, where do you go from here?

Throughout this book, there has been an emphasis on avoiding stultifying routines and replaying old habits. This is confirmed by research into longevity. For example, Marios Kyriasis, the founder of the British Longevity Society told the 'Sunday Times': *"If people are in a routine, neither the body nor brain is challenged. I also advise them to keep working for as long as possible, change jobs, take up new careers, or do part-time work in something which interests them." (24.04.11)*

A good place to start your action planning is to review where you are right now in your life in relation to the model below, based on work by Frederic Hudson (1999), but adapted for our purpose.

WHICH CHAPTER OF YOUR LIFE ARE YOU IN RIGHT NOW?

1. Phase 1: Go for it!

You may have recently started a new project, job, relationship or retirement, and you are fired up and excited by the new challenges this presents. You feel motivated, energised, working to achieve your goals, and achieving a measure of success.

2. Phase 2: The 'doldrums': stuck in the mud!

You feel 'bogged down,' restless, disenchanted, unfulfilled. You may be feeling trapped, angry, 'in a rut,' in decline, frustrated.

(If this is so, you need to find an 'exit plan.' Take time out to ponder and talk through your feelings and options with someone who is a good listener.)

OR, PERHAPS YOU ARE IN TRANSITION:

2. Phase 3: Cocooning:

You may have experienced an ending of some kind: retirement, relocation, redundancy, divorce, death of a loved one, etc. You are turning inwards to find new meaning and direction, plus a new sense of 'who you are' (as distinct from 'what you do').

(If you are here, give yourself time to be. Carefully consider your core values and your options, explore your creativity and take your time to incubate in your 'cocoon.')

4. **Phase 4: Get ready... get set...**

You are preparing yourself for the next phase of your life: researching to discover what might be available, seeking information, training, networking, building connections, discovering your options, and getting ready to face new challenges.

This is the best time to re-define your core values in relation to the next phase to achieve purpose, balance and a strong sense of your place in the world which is congruent with your self-identity. So, what are your priorities right now? (These may be quite different from your previous life priorities.)

- **Achievement?** Wanting to prove you 'can do it'? Leaving your 'mark' on the world?
- **Relationships?** New ones? Old ones? Seeking intimacy with someone special? Letting go of dysfunctional relationships? Mending bridges?
- **Play and creativity?** Needing to express yourself? Have fun? Feeling stifled right now? Wanting to be with creative people?
- **Personal identity?** Finding your 'true self' after years of being what everyone else wants you to be? Feeling as if you are living a lie? Who am I NOW?
- **Finding your purpose in life?** Your calling? 'Why am I here'? Wanting to feel more integrated and at peace within yourself? Seeking new direction or a new mission?
- **Giving back and serving?** Making a real difference to other people's lives? How can you give more to others through channelling your gifts and talents?

Which of these are you most attracted to?
What gives you a feeling of excitement or 'buzz'?
Which has least attraction for you?
Do any of them provoke a feeling of tension, discomfort or inner conflict?
Which do you feel 'neutral' towards?

You may find that different aspects of your life are in **different phases**. For example, you may be stuck in a rut at work (phase 2), but you have a new partner (phase 1). Or, the children have left home, and you need to reconstruct your life (phase 3). At the same time, you are maybe feeling unfulfilled professionally (phase 2).

Try to identify your **priorities** in relation to your core values and what seems to arouse most energy and interest for you. Make that your starting point for planning your goals.

Managing transitions

Following phase 4, we re-enter phase 1 but in a different light. There may be a complete transformation in our lives, or just a 'mini-transition' in one or two aspects. Whichever is the case, you will feel a new sense of purpose, energy and direction.

Drawing on William Blake's works, *'Songs of Innocence'* and *'Songs of Experience'*, Tony Buzan (2005) suggests that the whole of our lives is about transitional cycles. When we enter a new phase of 'innocence' (Phase 1: 'Go for it!') with the wide open eyes of a child, we feel curious, exploratory and ready to learn. Tony Buzan argues that approaching new cycles with 'renewed innocence' will re-awaken our creative energies, and this will help us to manage the transition to our advantage.

You may recall the joke that I recounted in Chapter 2: *'What's the difference between a groove and a grave? Only a matter of degree.'*

How easy it is to fall into the trap of suffering Phase 2 rather than taking the chance of trying something new. But, as I and other researchers have discovered, those who take the risk of finding new ventures find the benefits are immense. So, approach the 'golden chapter' as an exciting **new** adventure which can transform your life. Think of yourself as a chrysalis waiting to emerge as a butterfly, and take time to 'cocoon' yourself in order to prepare for the journey ahead.

Where will you start?

Perhaps you already have a clear idea of where to begin your planning. If not, the mind-map below, based on what I learned about the participants' thirst for novelty, may help you to consider a starting point which is right for you.

(I have left a couple of boxes blank for your own headings.)

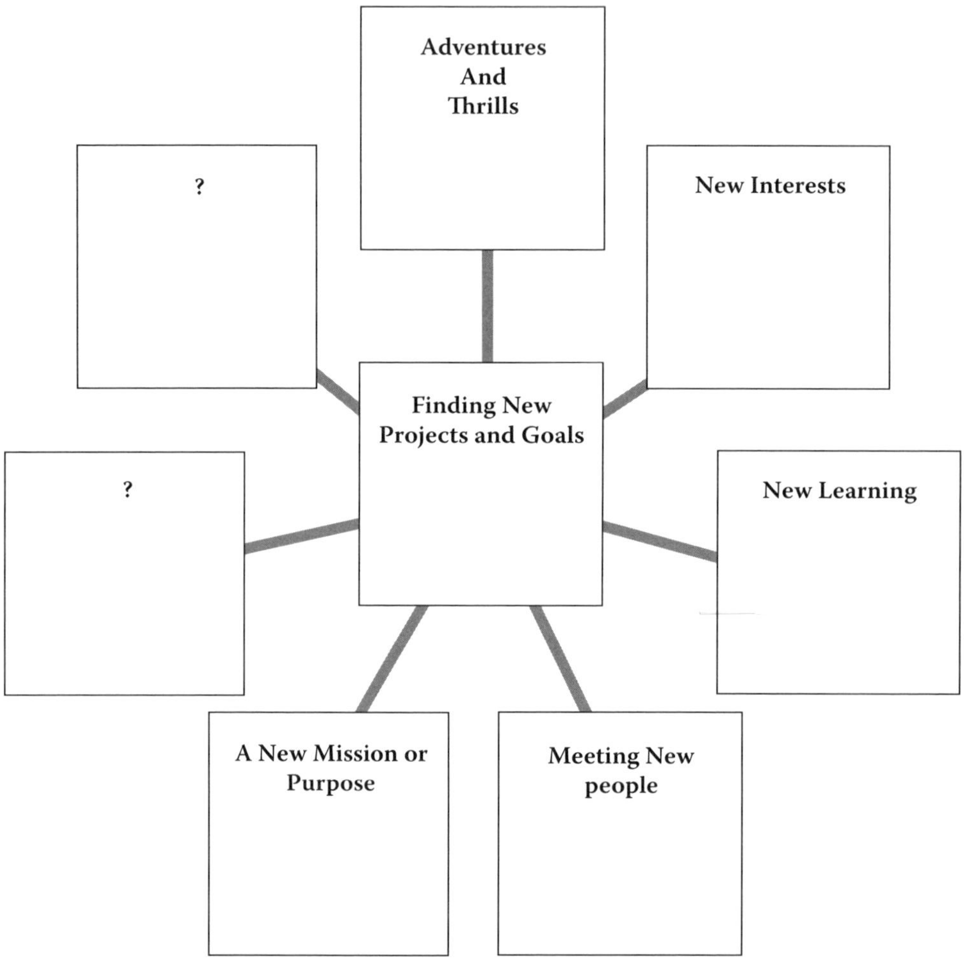

Some questions to address:

- **Use your signature strengths as starting points**. What are your gifts? Your dormant talents? What are you really good at?
- **What are you really interested in?**
- **What are your passions?**
- **What were your dreams as a child which you have not yet fulfilled?**
- **What is your 'unfinished business'** – something you had to abandon because other things got in the way, or you could not afford it?
- **Where will you find 'kindred spirits'** who may be very different from your work circles or family circles? Where are the people who share your core values and outlook on life? People with whom you feel a strong sense of connection?
- **Where do you feel most at ease and in tune with your real self?** The outdoors? Small groups? Working alone, or in a team? At home? Overseas?
- **What do you want to be remembered for? What is your legacy to the world?**

- ## What would you do if you let go of fear?

Visualise how it might be

Visualise your future scenario in detail. Your picture should encapsulate the way you would like your 'golden chapter' to be: focus only on your **positive** aspirations. It can be useful to draw or paint your ideas. (Don't worry about the artistic quality of the picture.) Alternatively, you can stick pictures cut out from magazines to create a collage of your vision. Use the images you are attracted to without questioning why. You may prefer to 'free-flow' on a large sheet of paper using key words and colours. There is no right or wrong way to do this. Don't stop to censor what you are attracted to- just trust your inner feelings and instincts, and analyse what the picture represents later.

Pin up the picture you have created somewhere so that you can see it, add to it, think about it and feel inspired by your dream. **Take time** (several days at least) to 'cocoon' and incubate your thoughts and ideas at this stage. Relax, close your eyes to see yourself succeeding, and loving every minute of your new ventures. Do this often until your conceptualisation begins to feel just right for you.

Set your goals and action plan

As Hudson (1999) correctly points out, our initial vision is rather blurred, indefinite and dream-like. Conversely, planning provides specific shape, deadlines and reality to the dream.

We need <u>both</u> in order to manage transitions effectively: first comes the dream and the vision, next, the plan. Many people fail because they never get beyond their hazy dreams.

So, when you feel ready, write a few goals which will address different areas of your life. Use the 'SMART' formula which we discussed in Chapter 4 for each goal. (Re-reading this section in Chapter 4 would be very useful at this stage.)

Specific
Measurable
Accountable
Realistic
Time bound

By.............................. (date), I will: ....
...
..

You will then be ready to devise an action plan which will take you into your future scenario. I would suggest that you choose one goal to start with. Perhaps you could select the goal which most excites you, or you feel will be easy to achieve.

Don't forget to keep your goal in SIGHT (e.g. your notice board or on a 'cue card'). Otherwise, it can slip 'off the radar'!

Then, complete your **ACTION PLANNER** overleaf which breaks your end goal into smaller, achievable, realistic steps with clear dates at each stage. Start with your end goal and work backwards. DO something today, however small. It is all too easy to procrastinate. Many people dream: few <u>achieve</u> their dreams because they never get around to DOING anything to turn their dreams into action.

STARTING POINT: WHAT WILL YOU DO TODAY?

DATE:

↓

SUB-GOAL: what I will have achieved by this date:

DATE:

↓

SUB-GOAL: what I will have achieved by this date:

DATE:

↓

SUB-GOAL: what I will have achieved by this date:

DATE:

↓

END GOAL: what I will have achieved by this date:

This will enhance my life by…

Date:

Be flexible, but be determined

Plans are organic documents, not set in stone. Evaluate your action plan frequently, and modify or adapt it as necessary. We can never fully predict what the future holds, and being too rigid may obstruct (or obscure) better opportunities which may arise. However, do not go to the other extreme and spend so much time continually reshaping and refining your plan that you don't get round to putting it into action at all.

As Dilts (1992) found in his study of elderly people who were vital and active, they all demonstrated a stubborn determination to achieve the goals they set for themselves. But, at the same time, they were flexible, and willing to 'roll with the punches' to implement their objectives. Furthermore, their goals were well defined and concrete, not 'woolly' or vague. (Hence our emphasis on 'SMART' goals.)

It's never too late

You may have some self-doubts along the way, or worry that you have left it too late to achieve your 'heyday'. So, stop for a minute to reflect on the things people achieve in their 'third age'. For example:

- Winston Churchill was Prime Minister in his late 70's
- Galileo wrote *'Dialogues Concerning the New Sciences'* when he was 72
- At 96, Enrico Paoli was still playing master-level chess
- Frank Lloyd Wright was 90 when he designed the Guggenheim Museum
- Benjamin Franklin designed bifocal spectacles at the age of 78
- Laura Ingalls Wilder published her *'Little House'* series in her 60's
- Picasso created some of his most vibrant, expressive works in his 80's
- Flora Thompson published the first volume of her trilogy, *'Lark Rise to Candleford,'* when she was 63
- Mary Wesley published her first novel for adults, *'Jumping the Queue,'* at the age of 71
- Alfred Wallis, the Cornish artist, did not start painting until he was in his 60's

In the words of George Eliot: ***'It's never too late to be who you might have been.'***

So, what is stopping you?

Start today- do something completely new, and, as Jim Beggs recommends, embrace your life!

And... start to sing about it!!!

Conclusion: Achieve Your Heyday, and Do It Your Own Way!

When I started to research this book, I must admit that I had a mixture of feelings about growing older. Like most people, I was looking forward to having more time to pursue interests and new ventures in my retirement, but, at the same time, images from the media conveyed a pretty bleak picture of old age. Is it all downhill after 60? Would I cope with the challenges ahead? What are the 'secrets' to ageing well and enjoying this chapter? Would it be 'golden', or a rather rusty brown?

So, how do I feel now? And, even more importantly, how do <u>you</u> feel after working your way through the book?

Undoubtedly there are challenges

As Bette Davis famously said: ***"Old age ain't no place for sissies."***

But, what I now realise is that, if we have faced previous challenges and traumas in our lives with a positive, strong attitude, we can deal with whatever lies ahead in the same way. When I talked to the participants about how they deal with the challenges of old age, they all told me that you gain an inner strength and resilience to cope.

So, take a moment to think about two or three problems, traumas, losses or blows you have experienced in your life. How did you cope with them? What strategies did you use? What did you learn? What do you do now that you were unable to do when you were 20 or 30? As we age, **we grow in experience and wisdom**. And, as we said in Chapter 1, these difficult times do enable us to develop resilience and coping mechanisms. What you learned from these experiences will help you to cope now and in the future, so, as Kate said with such passion: ***"Don't be afraid of old age- you <u>will</u> manage to deal with the challenges ahead."***

Incident	How you dealt with it	What you learned	How it helped you to grow	What you would do differently now

Work, self-discipline and effort are the keys

From my investigations, I totally agree with Ellen Langer (2010) who has researched the subject of ageing well extensively. She comments that we will all die one day, we don't really know what happens after we die, but, we do have some control over what happens right now in our lives.

Of course, there are no guarantees. But, being mindful, looking after your diet, exercise, thoughts, relationships, interests, brain, and so on, all pay dividends in our golden years. Our efforts **are** worthwhile as the evidence from the role models in my research, and other studies examined in the book, demonstrates.

All the participants have made, and are making, efficient, responsible life choices, and they are now reaping the benefits. That is not to say that they have no experience of illness, sadness or 'creaky bones,' but, they are still flourishing and enjoying their lives. It's certainly not all downhill for them!

I also find Marie de Hennezel (2011) reassuring when she writes that the life choices we make will influence how we enter old age. There are important decisions to be made and hard work to do if we are to enjoy that chapter of our lives.

Clearly, nobody can do this for us- the responsibility is ours. As the words of this popular quote remind us: ***'The trouble with life is that you're half way through it before you realise it's one of those 'do-it-yourself' affairs.'*** (Anon.)

Reap the rewards

If we do look after ourselves in body, mind, and spirit, the rewards are great. The participants told me of:

- feeling liberated from the burdens of work
- having fewer cares and worries
- enjoying time for hobbies and interests
- looking back with satisfaction at what they have achieved
- no longer feeling preoccupied about what other people think of them, and
- the opportunity to do new things which were unavailable before.

Again and again, they told me how 'lucky' they feel, and how important it is to savour each 'beautiful moment' in the day. Not once did I encounter self-pity, bitterness or resentment: what predominated is an appreciation of the gift of life. In Chrissie's words: *"Don't count the years, count your blessings."*

I have certainly learned the value of being fully present in the moment and counting my blessings every day since I started this project.

Still climbing

Several spoke of 'the privilege' to still be alive after the age of 70, and how important it is to see this golden chapter as a time for **continued** self-enrichment, both emotionally and spiritually. In other words, they believe they are not at the summit of what they can achieve yet!!

All too often, old age is portrayed by the media as a process of deterioration. But, as I and other researchers have found, there is development, growth, enrichment and an increase in wisdom which are all too often overlooked. Think of this time as an <u>ascent</u> to the summit of our lives, rather than a slippery slope downhill.

Accept and embrace the transition into old age

Each stage of our lives is marked by letting go of old things which no longer serve us well, and being open to the new growth which can develop if we embrace each chapter. At each transition, as we said in Chapter 10, there will be some transformation, because life itself is transient. Once we accept that fact with grace and fortitude, we can embark on this last journey with courage and enthusiasm.

All the participants have the serenity, the inner glow which comes with acceptance of both the positive features and the challenges that the third age can bring.

So, to get the best from this chapter, we need to consider what we will let go, in order to make room for new things, new experiences and new people to bring new energy into our lives. If we cannot adjust to this essential process, if we are always harping back to previous times when we used to do 'such and such', we will not only be consumed by bitterness and futile rebellion, we will also miss out on what we could **do** and **be** in our final chapter.

It is only by immersing ourselves in the process of positive change that we can gain access to the <u>deeper</u> dimension of who we really are.

So, what will you let go? What will you then take on your ascent into your new age?

In Chapter 10, you identified your goals in relation to your priorities. During this time of preparation for the last chapter of your life, it will be important to commit to your transition by carefully considering the following-

What (or who) will you let go ? What will you stop doing in order to make your transition into your new chapter?	
What (and who) will you hold on to?	
Which behaviours, people, dispositions, habits, etc will you take on the journey to the summit?	

Some questions to address:

What are some of the challenges you might face when 'letting go'?

Who and/or what will help you to stay strong on your ascent?

What will happen if you <u>don</u>'t let go?

What will happen if you do let go?

Which is preferable?

And, as our American friends say, "If you keep on doing what you've always been doing, you're gonna keep on getting what you've always been getting."

Put your affairs in order

According to 'Saga' magazine, a staggering 32% of 55-64 year-olds do not have a valid will. 56% of those questioned said they 'haven't got round to it yet'.

Which of these statements apply to you?

I have an up-to-date will [ ]

It is never too early to draw up a valid, updated will and to make all your important wishes known to those who will deal with your affairs. In addition, draw up a list of specific people whom you wish to receive personal gifts, and itemise what these are. Review and update this yearly, including the recipients' contact details.

Do not be tempted to do revengeful things via your 'last bequests'. How could that possibly bring you any serenity or inner peace?

You may also like to consider making a 'living will'. Your solicitor will help you with all these arrangements.

My funeral and burial arrangements are known to those who need to know [ ]

Discuss your preferred funeral and burial arrangements, and commit these to writing. Lodge them safely with your will which should be in a place known to your executers and nearest and dearest.

Outline your preferences for hymns, songs, music, readings, etc for your funeral. Do not make the mistake of assuming people will know what you would like to happen.

My wishes regarding organ donation are up to date [ ]

Ensure that your organ donor arrangements are updated, and that your family are aware of what you want to happen.

People know how much I have loved them, and how I value their contribution to my life [ ]

Write letters of gratitude which will bring comfort to those who receive them. Tell your loved ones often how much you love them.

'Putting your affairs in order' may appear morbid or unnecessary when you are younger, but, having lost close relatives and friends at an early age, I know from sad experience of the awful complications which can arise when there are no formal arrangements in place. I also know the abiding grief of not knowing if I was truly loved by them.

Think of the peace you will feel within when everything is in order and your wishes are known to those who matter to you.

A sense of completion

When I interviewed Shelagh, she talked at length about the *"inner peace"* she now feels. She said, *"There is a kind of quietness inside, a feeling that there is nothing more to strive for. But, I can look back at my life with a sense of fulfilment at what I have achieved, and many, many wonderful memories."*

She also spoke of a feeling of *"completion"*, and I was particularly interested in that, because I have known Shelagh for many years as a busy, hard-working business woman, always embarking on new ventures. But, how wonderful to feel so serene and at peace now she has reached the age of 84.

I hope I will feel the same, but I realise that, in order to arrive at this stage of completion, we must work hard to achieve our full potential first. Otherwise, our old age will be filled with resentment and regret at what we have not done with our lives, and all the missed opportunities we have shied away from along the way.

It is only by embracing challenges and taking calculated risks that we can finally gain that sense of inner serenity, content in the knowledge that we have arrived at the summit of our lives.

Reflection:

What are your 'must do's'- the things you know are essential if you are to achieve a sense of completion and inner peace later in your life?

Must Do's	When
•	
•	
•	
•	

These may include qualifications, careers, travel, creative outlets, writing, people you need to see, financial planning, running your own business, following a spiritual pathway- the choices are endless. Try to visualise yourself at Shelagh's age, looking back on your life and what you have done with it. What will bring the happiest memories, a sense of satisfaction, something to feel really proud of, knowing your life has made a difference in the world and to people who gain from your contribution?

Sometimes, when I engage in exercises like these with people, they are overwhelmed by feelings of modesty about their lives and what they can accomplish. If you feel like that, remember what Mother Teresa said when someone once criticised one of her projects, calling it a 'drop in the ocean'. ***"Yes, maybe,"*** she replied, ***"But every drop in the ocean is important."***

What will you be remembered for? What is your mission or reason for being here? It is never too early **or** too late to do something really worthwhile with your life.

A useful wake-up call can be to visualise your funeral and imagine what will be said at your eulogy. If there are gaps or things to amend, start today to put things right! Start living your eulogy now! And, remember, no one is going to put: *"She kept a very tidy, clean house"* on your gravestone!!!

Finally, do it <u>your way</u>:

In the introduction to this book, I quoted my dear friend, Michael Wilson, who said, *"There are at least 62 million people living in the UK. That means there are 62 million different ways of ageing well."*

I hope that you find **your own way** to your heyday as the unique, special individual that you are.

I hope that engaging with this book is giving you courage and optimism to embrace the golden chapter.

And, if there is 'another side', I hope we can all meet up there and **sing together** one day. What a wonderful choir we will be!

***'I have not come to resolve anything.
I have come to sing,
And for you to sing with me.'***

(Pablo Neruda, 1904-1973, Chilean poet and Nobel Prize Winner.)

Appendix 1: Baseline Questionnaire

Complete this before you read the book. This is will help you to see your current strengths and also your 'target' areas where improvement is desirable.

Chapter

1.	**When you are feeling a bit down, what do you do or say to yourself to feel more positive?**
2.	**What are THREE key things which give you a zest for life?** 1. 2. 3.
3.	**Looking good: On a scale of 1-10 (1 being not at all important), how important is daily personal grooming to you? [ ]**
	Why is that? **What do you like best about:** **Your face and skin-** **Your hair-** **Your body shape-** **Which colours suit you best NOW?**

	When did you last do a wardrobe 'audit'? Make-up audit? When did you last change your hairstyle or make-up?
4.	Exercise: Do you take regular exercise? How often do you exercise? What type/s of exercise do you take? What do you think are the benefits of exercise, physically and mentally?
5.	Diet and alcohol: How would you sum up your approach to eating and drinking? Are you happy with your weight?
6.	Socialising and relationships: Do you live alone? If so, do you converse with people every day? How often do you engage in planned social activity? What benefits do you derive from these activities? Who are you close to? Who could you call on in time of crisis? How many hugs have you given this week? And, how many have you received?

7.	**What do you currently do to keep your brain active? List all the activities you think are important to you:**
8.	**How is your memory?** **What do you remember easily?** **Are there any aspects of your memory that you are concerned about?**
9.	**Time management: Do you plan each day?** **What are your daily priorities? (e.g. clubs, outings, housework, cooking, massage, TV, courses, hobbies, walking- anything that is important to you)** **What benefits do you derive from these activities?** **What do you avoid?** **Why is that?** **Do you work? (This can include voluntary work/ Church work.)** **If so, what are the benefits?**
10.	**Which new projects and activities have you recently undertaken?** **And, why?** **What are your current goals in relation to getting the best out of your life?**

My Current Strengths	
Aspects to Improve	

After you have worked your way through the book and started to modify your lifestyle, complete Appendix 4: What You Have Achieved So Far.

Appendix 2 Eating and Drinking Record

(Photocopiable)

Date/ Time	What	Where	How	Why	How you felt afterwards	Strengths	Targets

What you learned from this exercise:

What you will eat/drink more of:

Less of:

Were your meals/snacks well-timed and spaced effectively? If not, what will you do differently?

Other thoughts:

Appendix 3: Monitoring Your Time, Thoughts and Feelings

(Photocopiable Record)

Date: Time:	What you are doing	In whose company (or alone)	Your thoughts and what you say to yourself	How you feel

Which patterns emerged from your record?

What have you learned from this exercise?

Appendix 4: Weekly Planner

(Photocopiable Chart)

a) Plan your 'must do' things first- work schedules, including charity and voluntary work, paid employment, appointments, bookings, classes, scheduled events, etc.

b) Then, plan your activities which will help you to 'flourish'- things which arouse positive emotions, engagement and flow; time with people who are uplifting and encouraging (i.e. 'radiators'); activities which give you a sense of meaning and purpose; goals which give you the satisfaction of accomplishment and achievement when you complete them. Refer back to Chapter 9 and the 'PERMA' acronym to remind you.

c) **Finally,** plan when to do your **'chores'.**

(There may be some overlap between a, b and c.)

Make a note of how you feel about what you have experienced at the end of each day.

	a.m.	p.m.	evening	Observations/ Feelings
Sunday				
Monday				
Tuesday				
Wednesday				
Thursday				
Friday				
Saturday				

Questions to ponder:

- **When/ where do you feel most in tune with your signature strengths and talents?**

- **And least?**

- **When/ where/ with whom do you feel most animated and energised? And least?**

- **When/ where/ with whom do you feel most drained of energy?**

Modify next week's activities accordingly until, week by week, by trial and error, you find a balance which works for YOU, as an individual. After about 5 or 6 weeks your new pattern will become established and you will begin to reap the benefits.

'We are what we repeatedly do.

Excellence, then, is not an act, but a habit.' (Aristotle)

Appendix 5: What You Have Achieved So Far

(Photocopiable Record)

Celebrate your achievements- no matter how small. Remember the proverb:

'A journey of 1,000 miles starts with the first step.'
(Lao-tzu, 604 B.C.- 531 B.C.)

So, record your successes against each goal you have set for yourself. Look at this page often because that will spur you on to live your life to the full and to take the best care of yourself that you can muster. Well done!!!

Chapter	Goals set	What you have achieved	What you will do next
1 Thinking			
2 Zest			
3 Appearance			
4 Exercise			
5 Diet/drinking			

Chapter	Goals set	What you have achieved	What you will do next
6 Relationships Socialising			
7 Brainpower			
8 Memory			
9 Time organisation			
10 New projects/ goals			
Conclusion Your summit			

Useful Contacts

www.ageuk.org.uk

Information and advice to help you make the most of your life and/or that of elderly relatives. This organisation is an amalgamation between Age Concern and Help The Aged.

Tel: 0800 169 6565

www.alzheimers.org.uk

Tel: 0845 300 0336

www.anxietyuk.org.uk

Anxiety UK

Tel: 0161 227 9898 or 08444 775 774

www.babcp.com

British Association for Behavioural and Cognitive Psychotherapies

Tel: 0161 705 4304- for list of accredited therapists

www.bacp.co.uk

British Association for Counselling and Psychotherapy

Tel: 01455 88 33 00

www.bap-psychotherapy.org

British Association of Psychotherapy

Tel: 0208 452 9823

www.b-eat.co.uk

BEAT Eating Disorders

Helpline: 0845 634 1414

www.carers.org.uk

For family carers

Tel: 0844 800 4361

www.citizensadvice.org.uk

Find your local branch in the telephone directory or your local library.

cliff@simplyimage.co.uk

Cliff Bashworth (MFIC)

www.simplyimage.co.uk

Tel: 01772 750052

www.colourmebeautiful.co.uk

To locate a CMB personal stylist.

020 76275211

www.crusebereavementcare.org.uk

Cruse Bereavement Care

Tel: (Help-line, daytime) 0844 477 9400

www.eating-disorders.org.uk

National Centre for Eating Disorders

Tel: 0845 838 2040

www.elderlyparents.org.uk

Information and advice for families of elderly parents

Tel: 0845 300 7585

www.extend.org.uk/classes

Tel: 01582 832760 or e-mail: admin@extend.org.uk

Details of chair based exercise classes for the over 60's or for those who are not so mobile.

If you are unable to attend a class, try the DVD, Move it or Lose it (£10 + £1.50 p&p)

www.moveitorloseit.co.uk

Tel: 0800 612 0450

If you live in the Scarborough area, and you prefer a one-to-one session, contact qualified Extend tutor, Ketyn Jepson.

Email: ketynjepson@yahoo.co.uk

www.foundationsuk.org

Eating Disorders information, support and treatment

Tel: 0845 291 0962

www.llttf.com

Living Life to the Full

(Free online practical exercises and activities to help change dysfunctional thinking patterns and get more out of your life.)

www.menieres.org.uk

Tel.: 0845 120 2975

The Meniere's Society can help with balance disorders and vertigo as well as Meniere's Disease and BPPV. Booklets on balance retraining and controlling your symptoms are available for a small charge.

www.relate.org.uk

Relate can help with all kinds of relationship problems, not just marriage and divorce.

Tel: 0300 100 1234 to find your nearest branch.

www.rockchoir.com

Find your nearest Rock Choir via the website, or-

Tel: 01252 714276

E-mail: office@rockchoir.com

www.thirdage.co.uk

For interesting, inspiring information for the over 50's.

www.turn2us.org.uk

A charity which can help you access money, welfare benefits and support in difficult times.

Tel: 0808 802 2000

www.u3a.org.uk

Tel: 020 8466 6139

To find out more about University of the Third Age, and to locate your nearest branch.

Sources and Useful Books for Further Reading

Texts referred to throughout the book:

De Hennezel, M. (2011) *The Warmth of the Heart Prevents Your Body from Rusting* (Rodale)

Dilts, R. et al. (1992) *NLP and Life Extension: Modelling Longevity* (Dynamic Learning Publications)

Doidge, T. (2007) *The Brain That Changes Itself* (Penguin Psychology)

Friedman, H. S. and Martin, L. R. (2011) *The Longevity Project: Surprising Discoveries for Health and Long Life* (Hay House)

Langer, E. (2010) *Counter Clockwise: A Proven Way to Think Yourself Younger and Healthier* (Hodder and Stoughton)

Strauch, B. (2010) *The Secret Life of the Grown-Up Brain* (Viking)

Wolpert, L. (2011) *You're Looking Very Well* (Faber and Faber)

Chapter specific texts and references you may wish to follow up:

Chapter 1: Manage Your Thinking

Briers, S. (2009) *How to Use CBT to Improve Your Mind and Your Life* (Prentice-Hall)

Schuller, Dr. R. (1983) *Tough Times Never Last, But Tough People Do* (Thomas Nelson)

Seligman, M. (2003) *Authentic Happiness* (Nicholas Brealey)

Taylor, S. (2011) *Out of the Darkness: From Turmoil to Transformation* (Hay House)

Chapter 2: Release Your Zest for Life

Csikszentmihalyi, M. (1990) *Flow: The Psychology of Optimal Experience, 1st Edition* (Harper and Row)

Drake, T. and Middleton, C. (2009) *You Can Be As Young As You Think* (Pearson)

Gawain, S. (1982) *Creative Visualisation* (Bantam)

Goleman, D. (1996) *Emotional Intelligence: Why It Can Matter More Than IQ* (Bloomsbury)

Hepworth, B. in Read, H., Ed. (1934) *Unit One,* Subtitled, *'The Modern Movement in English Architecture, Painting and Sculpture'* (Cassell and Company Ltd.)

Jeffers, S. (1987) *Feel the Fear and Do It Anyway* (Arrow)

Chapter 3: Enjoy the Way You Look at Any Age

Colour Me Beautiful (2008) *Colour Me Younger* (Hamlyn)

I hate the title, but the book does contain some excellent tips and advice, all illustrated by real-life models aged 40, 50, 60 and beyond.

Other titles by CMB include: *'Colour Me Confident', 'Colour Me Slimmer' and 'Image Matters for Men'.*

Chapter 4: Keep Moving

Egan, G. (1990) *The Skilled Helper* (Brooks/Cole)

Katzmarzyk, P. (Professor at Pennington Biomedical Research Centre, Louisiana) cited in *'The Times'*, 19.03. 2011: *'What really makes you live longer?'*

Lewin, K. (1947) 'Frontiers in group dynamics', *Human Relations,* vol. 1, no. 1, pp. 5- 41

Veerman, J. L. (et al.) (15 August, 2011, online) 'Television Viewing Time and Reduced Life Expectancy: A Life Table Analysis', *British Journal of Sports Medicine*

(Online at: www.bjsm.bmj.com, last accessed 17 August, 2011)

Chapter 5: A Little Bit of What You Fancy...

Lawson, T. (2011) *A Year in the Village of Eternity* (Bloomsbury)

Oxford Project to Investigate Memory and Ageing ('OPTIMA'): http://www.medsci.ox.ac.uk/optima (Last accessed 17 August, 2011)

Rotter, J. (1966) *The Locus of Control,* available from: http://www.psych.uncc.edu/pagoolka/LocusofControl-intro.html (Last accessed 20 July, 2011)

Details of Dr. Weili Xu's research can be found on: http://yalemedicalgroup.org under the heading: *'Extra Pounds at Mid-life May Boost Dementia Risk Later'*

Chapter 6: Cultivate Good Relationships and an Uplifting Social Life

Drake, T. and Middleton, C. (2009) *You Can Be as Young as You Think* (Prentice Hall)

Seligman, M. (2011) *Flourish: A New Theory of Positive Psychology* (Simon and Schuster)

Chapters 7 and 8: Brain and Memory Strategies

Bragdon, A. and Gamon, D. (2010) *Use It or Lose It* (Geddes and Grosset)

Buzan, T. (1992) *Use Your Memory* (BBC Books) Tony Buzan has also published other very useful books on mind maps, learning foreign languages, etc.

Fulghum, R. (2007) Essay: *Dancing the Dances As long As I Can* (in *'This I Believe 2'*, Allison, J. and Gediman, D., Eds. (2009)) Holt/ Macmillan.

This inspiring essay can also be downloaded from various websites including: http://www.uuacsherborn.org/sermons/nov152009.pdf

O'Brien, D. (2000) *Learn to Remember* (Duncan Baird Publishers) – Dominic O'Brien has written several other books about memory

Raugh, M.R. and Atkinson, R.C. (1975) *'A Mnemonic Method for Learning a Second Language', Journal of Educational Psychology,* vol. 67, pp. 1-16

Chapter 9: Manage Your Time Effectively

Covey, S. (1989) *The Seven Habits of Highly Effective People* (Simon & Schuster)

Dickson, A. (1982) *A Woman in Your Own Right* (Quartet Books)

Dryden, W. and Constantinou, D. (2004) *Assertiveness Step by Step* (Sheldon Press)

Seligman, M. (2011) *Flourish: A New Theory of Positive Psychology* (Simon and Schuster)

Chapter 10: Find New Projects and Goals

Buzan, T. (2005) *Buzan's Embracing Change* (BBC Worldwide Learning)

Fulghum, R. (2007) Essay: *Dancing the Dances As long As I Can* (in *'This I Believe 2'*, Allison, J. and Gediman, D., Eds., 2009, Holt/Macmillan)

Hudson, F. M. (1999) *The Handbook of Coaching* (Jossey Bass)

Kyriasis, M. interviewed in *'The Sunday Times'* (24.04.2011): *'Life Begins at 90'*

If you are thinking of changing careers, or considering some part-time or voluntary work, try:

Bolles, R.N. (2011) *What Color Is Your Parachute? A Practical Manual for Job-Hunters and Job Changers* (Ten Speed Press/ Random House)

If you are 'stuck in a rut' and afraid of change:

Johnson, S. (1999) *Who Moved My Cheese?* (Vermilion) may be just what you need to nudge you into taking control of your life.

Topic Index